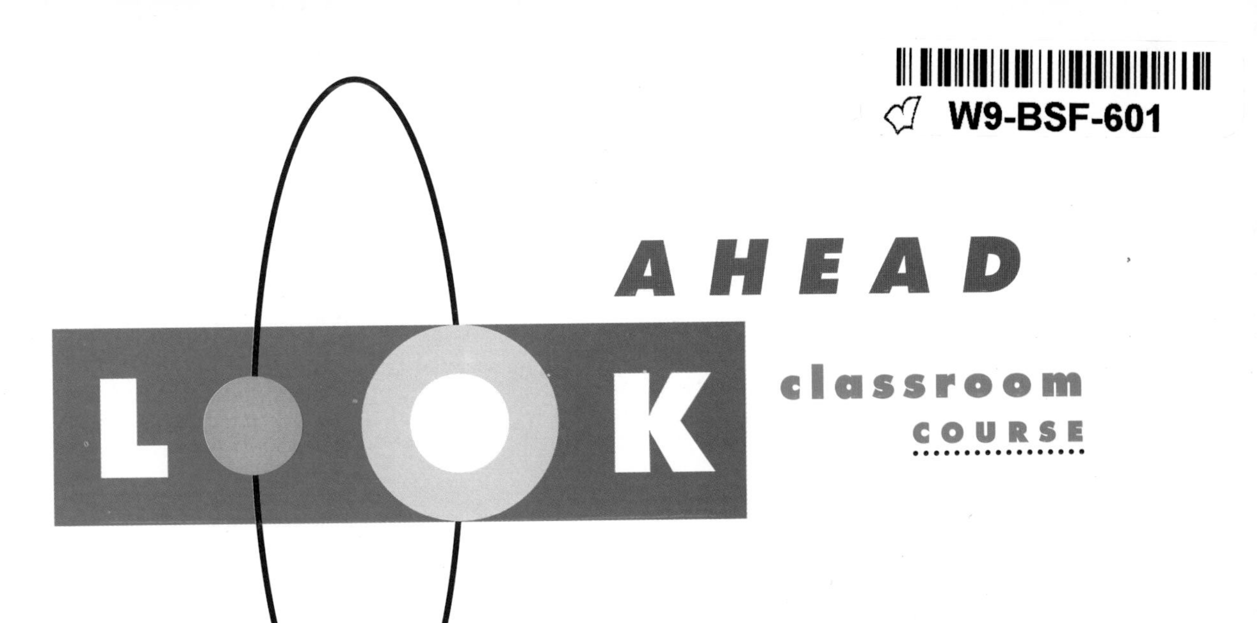

STUDENTS' BOOK 1

ANDY HOPKINS
JOCELYN POTTER

Look Ahead: a partnership between

BBC English

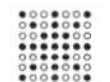
The British Council

University of Cambridge Local Examinations Syndicate (UCLES)

Longman ELT

with the cooperation of the Council of Europe

Longman

FUNCTIONS	READING / WRITING	COMPARING CULTURES
		International words
Greeting Introducing Thanking Asking meaning Talking about places Buying things Asking prices	R: Hotel publicity leaflet W: Sentences: personal information Descriptions of objects	
Asking for personal information Asking about jobs Spelling	R: Job advertisements Job descriptions W: Completing a form Address on an envelope Paragraph: personal information Making corrections	Surnames related to jobs Ways of writing addresses
Greeting Leaving Asking for repetition Asking about people Asking someone's age Asking about colour	R: Tickets, cards, etc. W: Sentences: personal information List	Ways of meeting and leaving Colours of familiar objects
Asking what someone wants Asking about food Talking about prices Asking for something Describing what there is	R: Menu Restaurant Guide W: Shopping list Fax Punctuation	Dishes from different countries
Describing places to live Talking about rates Saying you do not understand	R: Brochure Flat advertisements Description of rooms Information on houses Chart W: Paragraph about a person's life Descriptions of a hotel, a typical house	Varieties of language Rooms, furniture, living habits
Describing family relationships Talking about jobs Talking about dates/birthdays Asking about and giving opinions of people and objects Describing people	R: Text: personal information Descriptions of people Article about families W: Descriptions of people Information about a person	Family size Age of leaving home
Responding to thanks Specifying particular things Asking for something in a shop Asking for clarification	R: Shop advertisements W: Shopping list Packing list	Shops Polite language for shopping

FUNCTIONS	READING/WRITING	COMPARING CULTURES
Telling the time Talking about routines Talking about frequency	R: Short texts about routines Text on changing the clocks A brochure W: Sentences: comparing routines Formal letter asking for information	Use of 24-hour clock Changing the clocks
Talking about likes and dislikes Giving opinions Talking about time duration Talking about present activities	R: Poster Graph Comments on leisure activities Holiday advertisement W: Information about viewing habits Description Formal letter	Watching TV
Talking about abilities Talking about working hours	R: Texts about jobs W: Message Short text about your working day Short text about a job Improving a text	Working and opening hours
Talking about past experiences Giving opinions Describing places Talking about the weather	R: Informal letter Postcard Guidebook extract W: Descriptions of holidays Postcard Text about a famous building	Ways of ending informal letters or postcards
Talking about dates and places of birth Saying when something happened Warning someone	R: Articles Biography in note form W: Form Short biography	
Inviting/Accepting/Refusing/ Thanking Making polite requests Offering Talking about quantity Asking permission	R: Informal invitations and reply Place settings Restaurant signs A recipe W: Informal invitations and reply Comparing habits A recipe	Eating at someone's house Place settings Eating and sleeping times
Asking about location Asking for and giving directions Talking about distances Giving instructions Making polite requests	R: Informative articles Accommodation booking form W: Paragraph about driving habits Accommodation booking form Instructions	Driving on left/right Miles/kilometres Derivation of some street names
Making suggestions Accepting/refusing a suggestion Offering Talking about future arrangements	R: Advertisements Informal letter The beginning of a play W: Film/TV review Improving a text Informal letter Script	Film certificates

Welcome to English!

1 **You probably already know some words used in English. How many of these do you know? Match the words with the pictures.**

Picture 1: pizza, coffee ...

radio	sandwich	jeans	rock music	piano
pizza	jazz	lemonade	video cassette	disco
coffee	toilet	hotel	CD	salad	restaurant
reception	computer	saxophone	guitar	
cassette	television	hamburger	telephone	
chips	camera	violin		

COMPARING CULTURES

2 **Which words are the same in your language?**

3 **Which words are nearly the same?**

4 **Now work in pairs. Make a list of any other English words you know.**

3
HILTON INTERNATIONAL
JUL 365K
WORLDWIDE RESERVATIONS
TRUSTHOUSE FORTE HOTELS
4
DR180

1 International English

At the airport

Focus

- Names
- Countries
- Nationalities
- Capital cities

- Greeting
- Introducing
- Thanking
- Asking meaning

- Verb *to be* (singular): *am ('m), are, is ('s)*
- Pronouns: *I, you*
- Possessive adjectives: *my, your*
- Demonstrative pronoun: *this*
- Questions: *What?, Where?*
- Preposition: *from* + country/city

1 Listen and read. James Brady is in Ireland.

1 WOMAN: Good morning.
JAMES: Good morning.
WOMAN: What's your name, please?
JAMES: Brady. James Brady.
WOMAN: Right. Here you are, Mr Brady.
JAMES: Thank you.

2 JAMES: Where are you from?
TERESA: I'm from Spain – from Madrid. And you?
JAMES: Ireland. I'm from Dublin.

3 TERESA: This is Marco.
JAMES: Hello. My name's James.
MARCO: Hi.
TERESA: And I'm Teresa.

2 Ask and answer about names.

A: *Hello. What's your name?*
B: *My name's Dino.*

3 Tell the class your name and introduce your friend.

My name's Ulrike. This is Dino.

4 Match the capital cities with the countries. Then listen and check your answers.

Dublin – Ireland

CAPITAL	COUNTRY
1 Dublin	Japan
2 Rome	Spain
3 Cairo	Britain
4 Paris	Poland
5 Madrid	Greece
6 Washington	Italy
7 Berlin	Egypt
8 Ankara	Ireland
9 London	Brazil
10 Athens	Germany
11 Tokyo	Turkey
12 Brasilia	Portugal
13 Lisbon	France
14 Warsaw	the United States (of America)

5 Listen again and repeat. Then tell the class the names of other countries you know.

6 Ask and answer about people's names and countries.

Marco/Rome

A: *What's your name?*
B: *My name's Marco.*

A: *Where are you from?*
B: *I'm from Italy.*

1 Teresa/Madrid
2 Anna/Warsaw
3 Nilgun/Ankara
4 Noriko/Tokyo
5 Samir/Cairo
6 Paul/London
7 Luis/Brasilia
8 Cristina/Athens
9 Mario/Lisbon
10 Ulrike/Berlin

7 Listen and read. James Brady is in Britain now.

MAN: Excuse me. What does 'EC' mean?
JAMES: It means 'European Community'. What nationality are you?
MAN: I'm Brazilian.
JAMES: OK. Desk 2.
MAN: Thank you.

8 Pronunciation. Listen and repeat the nationalities.

COUNTRY	NATIONALITY	COUNTRY	NATIONALITY
1		3	
Britain	British	Brazil	Brazilian
Ireland	Irish	Egypt	Egyptian
Poland	Polish	Italy	Italian
Spain	Spanish	Germany	German
Turkey	Turkish	the United States	American
2		4	
Japan	Japanese	France	French
Portugal	Portuguese	Greece	Greek

9 Stress and intonation. Listen and repeat.

What's your name?

Where are you from?

What nationality are you?

10 Work in pairs.

Student A: Look at the desk signs in Exercise 7. Ask about nationality and say which desk to go to.
Student B: You are one of the people in Exercise 6.

A: *What nationality are you?*
B: *I'm Italian.*
A: *OK. Desk 1.*
B: *Thank you.*

11 Write sentences for three of the people in Exercise 6.

My name's Marco. I'm Italian. I'm from Rome.

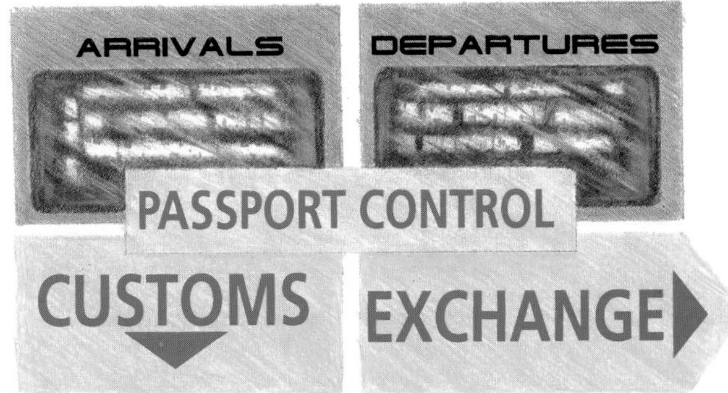

12 Look at the airport signs above. Ask what they mean.

A: *Excuse me. What does 'Arrivals' mean?*
B: *It means . . .*

Focus

- Facilities
- Numbers 1–10
- Money
- Further practice: cities

- Talking about places
- Buying things
- Asking prices
- Leaving
- Further practice: thanking, asking meaning

- *I'd like …*
- Question: *How much?*
- Pronoun: *it*
- Plural: + *s*
- Adverb: *there*
- Preposition: *in* + language
- Further practice: verb *to be*, questions: *Where?, What?*

Airport facilities

1 Listen and read.

1 TERESA: Excuse me. Where's the bank?
MAN: It's there.
TERESA: Thank you.

2 WOMAN: Excuse me. Where's Gate 10?
MARCO: Sorry, I don't know.

2 Ask and answer about other places at the airport. Look at the map and point to the correct place when you answer.

A: *Excuse me. Where's the café?*
B: *It's there.*
A: *Thank you.*

3 Look at the gate numbers. Listen and repeat.

Gates 1, 2, 3, 4, 5 ←

Gates 6, 7, 8, 9, 10 →

4 Write these numbers in the correct order.

six three two five four eight ten nine seven one

5 Listen to the announcements. Complete the chart with the names of the cities. Choose from this list:

Mexico City Ankara Lisbon Rome Prague Tokyo Berlin Madrid Athens Paris London Singapore Amsterdam

DEPARTURES		
Flight number	To	Gate number
AF 421	*Paris*	*6*
IB 386	.....	.....
OK 292	.....	.....
BA 654	.....	.....
KL 197	.....	.....
MX 578	.....	.....
AZ 963	.....	.....

Listen again. Write the gate numbers.

6 Listen and read.

MARCO: Er, I'd like this T-shirt, please. How much is it?
ASSISTANT: Eight pounds.
MARCO: Eight pounds. Here you are.
ASSISTANT: Thank you.
MARCO: Thanks. Goodbye.
ASSISTANT: Goodbye.

DISCOVERING LANGUAGE

7 Look at the money below. What is the rule for making plurals of regular nouns?

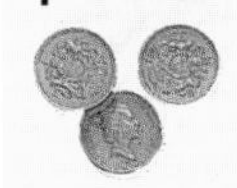

£1 one pound (a pound)
£2 two pounds
£3 three pounds

$1 one dollar (a dollar)
$2 two dollars
$3 three dollars

8 Work in pairs.

Student A: Buy things from your partner's shop. Use the picture and the dialogue from Exercise 6.
Student B: You are a shop assistant. Turn to page 116.

9 Pronunciation. Listen to the words 1–5. Then match the words a–e with the vowel sounds.

please – 5

1 /æ/ bag — a) please
2 /ɑː/ bar — b) thank
3 /e/ ten — c) it
4 /ɪ/ six — d) France
5 /iː/ three — e) French

10 Work in pairs. Test your partner. Ask and answer about the objects below.

Student A: Look at the pictures. Answer your partner's questions.
Student B: Turn to page 116. Ask questions.

B: *Number one. What's this?*
A: *Is it a book?*
B: *Yes, it is./No, it isn't. It's a passport.*

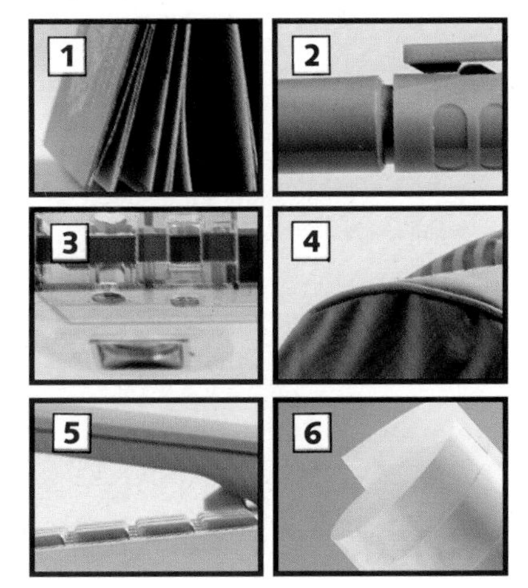

11 Now write a sentence to describe each picture.

1 It's a passport.

ENGLISH AROUND YOU

What's this in English?
It's a pizza!
MENU

Development

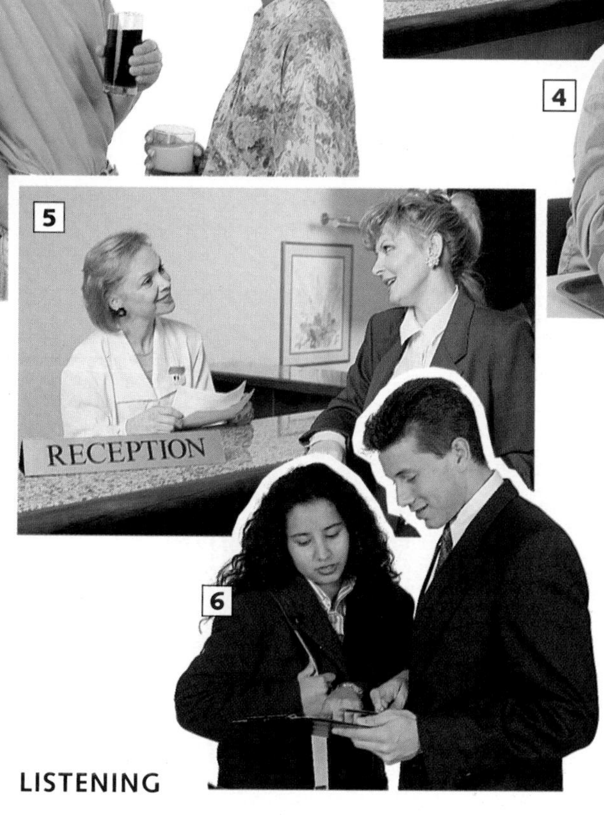

LISTENING

1 Look at the pictures and listen to the six conversations. Complete the chart with the correct numbers and countries.

PICTURE	NAME	COUNTRY
.....	Paula da Costa	.....
.....	Krystyna Nowak	.....
one	Wu Jiang	*China*
.....	Pietro Rossi	.....
.....	Jeff Adams	.....
.....	Sumiko Ito	.....

SPEAKING

2 Tell your partner about the people above. Point to the person you are talking about.

This is Wu Jiang from China.

3 Work in pairs. Test your partner. Ask and answer about famous places.

Student A: Look at the pictures below. Ask your partner about each place.
Student B: Turn to page 116. Ask your partner about the country.

A: Number one. What's this?

B: It's the Eiffel Tower.
A: Yes, that's right.

B: Sorry, I don't know.
A: It's the Eiffel Tower.

B: Where is it?

A: It's in France.
B: Yes, that's right.

A: Sorry, I don't know.
B: It's in France.

1 the Eiffel Tower

2 Big Ben

3 the White House

4 the Great Wall

5 the Taj Mahal

6 Mount Fuji

WRITING: Sentences

4 Make sentences from the words below.

What's your name?

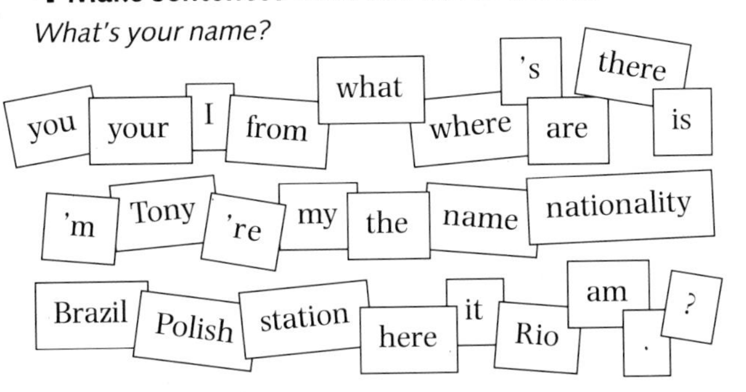

5 Write three sentences about yourself. Write about your name, your town/city and your nationality.

READING

6 Read this advertisement for a hotel in London. Look at the symbols for the facilities below and label them. Then write *Yes* or *No* for each facility.

1 – *bar* – *Yes*

Kensington Hotel
A family hotel with reasonable prices, thirty minutes from Heathrow Airport.
Rooms from £62 (single) £85 (double).
Prices include full English breakfast and VAT.
Facilities
All rooms have a private bathroom, a telephone and a colour television.
Meals are available in the restaurant.
Light snacks are served all day in the bar.
Souvenir shop.
Kensington Road, London W8 6PE Tel. 071 222 1592

 1 *bar*

 2 *swimming pool*

 3 *tennis court*

   4 .....

 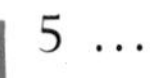 5 .....

 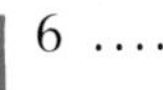 6 .....

 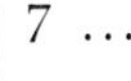 7 .....

  8 .....

 9 .....

Summary

FUNCTIONAL LANGUAGE

Talking about names, countries and nationalities
What's your name?
My name's Luis.
Where are you from?
I'm from Brazil.
What nationality are you?
I'm Brazilian.

Talking about places
Excuse me. Where's the bank?
It's there./Sorry, I don't know.
Where's Big Ben?
It's in Britain.

Talking about objects
What's this?
Is it a book?
Yes, it is./No, it isn't.
It's a passport.

Greeting someone
Good morning.
Hello./Hi.

Introducing someone
This is Teresa.

Thanking someone
Thank you./Thanks.

Leaving someone
Goodbye.

Asking about meaning
What does 'EC' mean?
It means . . .
What's this in English?

Using numbers
one – ten

Buying things
I'd like this T-shirt, please.
Here you are.

Asking about prices
How much is it?

GRAMMAR

The verb *to be*: present simple tense (part)

AFFIRMATIVE

FULL FORM	SHORT FORM
I am	I'm
you are	you're
it is	it's

Pronouns
I you it

Articles
a book the Eiffel Tower

Zero article
+ cities/countries/languages (*from Paris/in France/in English*)

Question words
What? Where?
How much?

Singular and plural + *s*
pound pounds

Prepositions
from Brazil/Paris
in France *in* English

Possessive adjectives
my your

Demonstrative pronoun
this

Adverb
there

Modal: *'d*
I'd like

See the Grammar Reference section at the back of the book for more information.

2 Information

Personal information

Focus

- Addresses
- Telephone numbers
- Alphabet
- Further practice: names
- Spelling
- Question: *How?*
- Pronouns: *he, she*
- Possessive adjectives: *his, her*
- Preposition: *in* + city/town
- Possessive *'s*
- Verb *to be* (singular) short answers

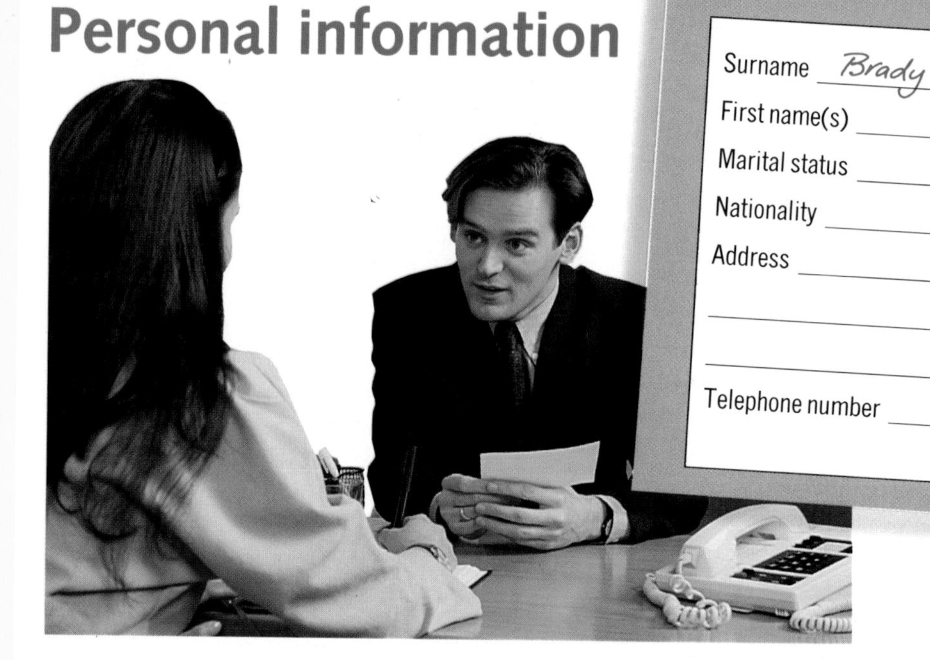

Marketing
Advertising
Publicity

Surname *Brady*
First name(s) ______
Marital status ______
Nationality ______
Address ______
______
______
Telephone number ______

1 Listen and read. James Brady is starting a new job with MAP Advertising. The name of his boss is Tom Hall. Tom Hall's secretary, Rita, is checking James's details.

RITA: Now, Mr Brady. Surname 'Brady', B-R-A-D-Y.
JAMES: Yes.
RITA: Your first name is James?
JAMES: Yes.
RITA: Are you married or single?
JAMES: Single.
RITA: And you're from Ireland.
JAMES: Yes.
RITA: What's your address in London?
JAMES: The Birch Hotel, Maysoule Street, M-A-Y-S-O-U-L-E, London E1.
RITA: What's the telephone number?
JAMES: 352 0529.

2 Listen and read again, and complete the form.

3 Say the telephone numbers.

30611 – *Three oh six double one.*

947 1122 0865 688592 844042
56321 071 405 9529 358002

4 Listen and repeat the alphabet.

Aa Bb Cc Dd Ee Ff Gg Hh Ii
Jj Kk Ll Mm Nn Oo Pp Qq Rr
Ss Tt Uu Vv Ww Xx Yy Zz

5 Find four words in Unit 1. Ask your partner to spell them.

A: *How do you spell 'diary'?*
B: *D-I-A-R-Y.*

6 Interview your partner. Ask questions and note the answers.

... surname?
What's your surname?
How do you spell it?

... surname?
... first name?
... married or single?
... nationality?
... address?
... telephone number?

7 Listen and read. James is talking to his sister, Rosie. She lives in Brighton. Write the names and nationalities of three people who work at MAP Advertising.

ROSIE: Hello, 32294.
JAMES: Hello, Rosie. This is James.
ROSIE: Hi, James. Where are you?
JAMES: I'm in London.
ROSIE: Oh, good! How's your new job?
JAMES: Oh, it's OK. Everyone's very friendly. Tom Hall – my boss – is the managing director. He's American. And Rita's very nice. She's Tom's secretary.
ROSIE: Is Rita American too?
JAMES: No, she isn't. She's from London.

DISCOVERING LANGUAGE

8 Read about Jeff and Pilar. What are the rules for *he, she, his* and *her*?

His name's Jeff.
He's American.

Her name's Pilar.
She's Mexican.

9 Now tell the class about your partner. Use your notes from Exercise 6.

His/Her surname is ...

10 Complete the conversations.

1 Rosie is talking to her friend Maria about James.

ROSIE: (1) ..... brother's in England!
MARIA: Oh, good! Is (2) ..... in Brighton?
ROSIE: No, (3) ..... isn't. (4) .....'s in London.
MARIA: What's (5) ..... name?
ROSIE: James.
MARIA: Is (6) ..... single?
ROSIE: Yes, (7) ..... is.

2 James is talking to Rita about Rosie.

JAMES: (1) ..... sister's in England too.
RITA: Oh. Is (2) ..... in London?
JAMES: No, (3) ..... isn't. (4) ..... job's in Brighton.
RITA: What's (5) ..... name?
JAMES: Rosie.
RITA: Is (6) ..... single?
JAMES: Yes, (7) ..... is.

DISCOVERING LANGUAGE

11 Read the sentences below. What is the rule for the possessive *'s*?

I'm Marco**'s** friend.
This is Rosie**'s** diary.
She's Tom**'s** secretary.

12 Now ask and answer.

Rita/Tom/secretary?
A: *Is Rita Tom's secretary?*
B: *Yes, she is./No, she isn't.*

1 James/Rosie/brother?
2 Rosie/Maria/sister?
3 James/Tom/boss?
4 Tom/Rosie/boss?
5 Tom/Rita/boss?

ENGLISH AROUND YOU

Jobs

1 Match the words below with the people in the picture.

a shop assistant – K

1 a shop assistant	6 a builder	11 a cleaner
2 an electrician	7 a doctor	12 a driver
3 a mechanic	8 an actor	13 an artist
4 a secretary	9 a teacher	14 a nurse
5 a musician	10 a painter	

Focus

- Jobs
- Articles: *a, an*
- Further practice: verb *to be* (singular) short answers, possessive *'s*
- Further practice: pronouns: *I, you, he, she*

DISCOVERING LANGUAGE

2 Look at the words for jobs above. What is the rule for *a* and *an*?

3 Pronunciation. Listen and read. Notice the /ə/ sound for *er/or* at the end of a word.

actor builder driver teacher doctor painter

Listen again and repeat.

4 Stress and intonation. Listen and repeat.

What's your job? I'm an actor.
What's her job? She's a doctor.
What's his job? He's a teacher.

5 Ask and answer about the people in the picture.

A: *What's B's job?*
B: *He's a builder.*
A: *Is F a nurse?*
B: *No, she isn't. She's a doctor.*
A: *Is L an electrician?*
B: *Yes, he is.*

6 Work in pairs.

Student A: Act out a job in the picture.
Student B: Guess the job.

A: *What's my job?*
B: *Are you a cleaner?*
A: *Yes, I am./No, I'm not.*

7 **Ask and answer about each other. Then ask about your partner's mother, father, brother and sister.**

A: *What's your job?*
B: *I'm a ...*
A: *What's your mother's job?*
B: *She's a ...*

8 **Listen to two people talking about jobs. Write the jobs you hear.**

9 **Read about Boris Yeltsin and then write about one man and one woman in the pictures. Then write about yourself or someone in your family.**

Boris Yeltsin
Russia
politician

His name is Boris Yeltsin.
He is Russian.
He is a politician.

1 Whoopi Goldberg
the United States
actress

2 Paul Gascoigne
Britain
footballer

3 Steffi Graf
Germany
tennis player

4 Julio Iglesias
Spain
singer

COMPARING CULTURES

10 **These surnames are also the names of jobs. Match the names with the pictures. Use a dictionary to help you. Which surnames in your country are also the names of jobs?**

Picture 1 – thatcher

Margaret THATCHER Leslie COOK Tony BAKER Fay BUTCHER Penny CARPENTER

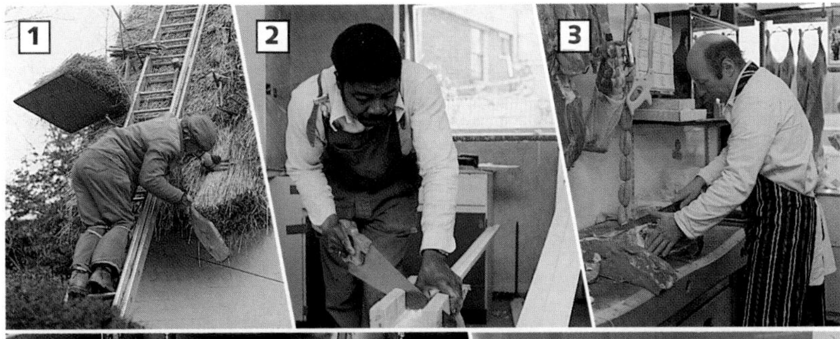

Development

READING

1 Look at the advertisements. Answer the questions about each advertisement.

What is the job?
Receptionist.

1 What is the job?
2 Where is the company?
3 What is the name of the company?
4 What is the salary for the job?

JOBSEARCH

JOBS IN THE SOUTH-EAST

Receptionist
A & E Jones Limited is looking for a receptionist to start immediately.
Salary £6 an hour.
Telephone Brighton 34211 for more information.
A&E Jones
BUILDERS

SATURDAY JOB
Cleaner (16+) for company in Hove. 8 a.m.–1 p.m. only. £5 an hour.
Contact the Manager, Property First, 49, London Road, Hove.

COMPUTER OPERATOR
wanted for a small holiday company in Eastbourne.
£9 an hour
(20 hours a week).
Contact Judy Phillips at
BEST HOLIDAYS
112, Market Street, Eastbourne.

SPORTSWEAR
Are you young, dynamic and intelligent? You can earn £7 an hour as assistant manager of a small sports shop in Hove.
Phone Sportswear on 0273 31100 today!

JOBS ABROAD

Summer in the USA
Spend nine weeks at an American teenage summer camp as a sports teacher (tennis, football, golf).
$20 a week pocket money, all food and accommodation provided.
For an application form, send a postcard with your name and address to: Camp California, 1022 Marine Drive, San Diego, California 921081, USA.

LISTENING

2 Amanda is the manager of a job centre. She interviews people for jobs. Listen to her interview with Susan and complete the chart with the correct information.

First name	.....
Surname	......
Title	*Miss*
Marital status	.....
Address	.....
	Harrow,
	Middlesex
Telephone number	.....
Nationality	.....

SPEAKING

3 Check your answers to Exercise 2 with your partner.
Is her first name . . . ?

4 Check the spelling of difficult words on the chart. Ask your teacher.

COMPARING CULTURES

5 Look at Amanda's office address on the envelope. What are the differences from addresses in your country?

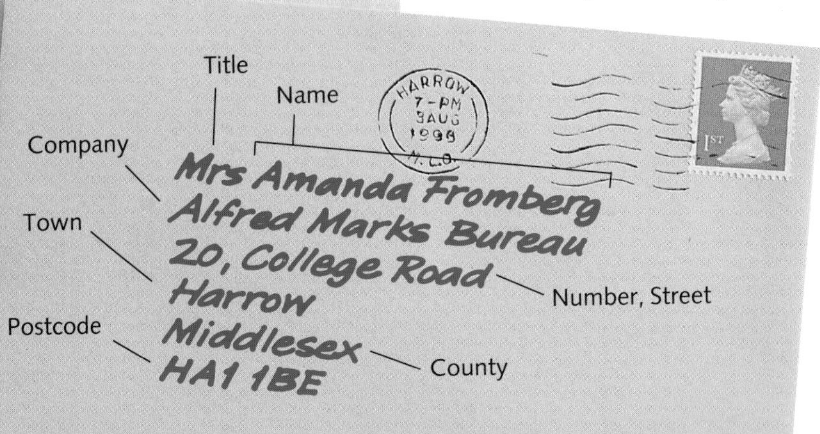

WRITING: An address

6 Look again at your information about Susan from Exercise 2. Write Susan's address on an envelope.

READING

7 Read the texts and name the jobs.

Jane works in a school. She speaks to students. She uses a book called *Look Ahead.*

She's a teacher.

1 Ricky works in a shop. He sells books, cassettes, posters and pens.

2 Simon works in an office. He uses a computer and a fax machine. He writes letters for his boss.

3 Helen works in a hospital. She gives medicines to patients.

WRITING: Personal information

8 Write a paragraph about your partner. Start like this:

His/Her name is . . .

WRITING: Corrections

9 Read the paragraph below. Notice the grammar and spelling mistakes. Then check your partner's paragraph from Exercise 8. Correct the grammar and spelling mistakes.

is
Her name Anna Gtazek.
Polish
She's Poland. Her address

is Studencka, 27, Gdansk.
Her telephone
His telefon number in

Gdansk is 751122.

Summary

FUNCTIONAL LANGUAGE

Asking for personal information
What's your first name?
Are you married?
What's your address?
What's your telephone number?

Using titles
Mr Mrs Miss

Asking about jobs
What's your job?
I'm a musician.

Asking how to spell a word
How do you spell 'James'?

GRAMMAR

The verb *to be*: the present simple tense – singular

AFFIRMATIVE		NEGATIVE	
FULL FORM	SHORT FORM	FULL FORM	SHORT FORM
I am	I'm	I am not	I'm not
you are	you're	you are not	you aren't
he is	he's	he is not	he isn't
she is	she's	she is not	she isn't
it is	it's	it is not	it isn't

INTERROGATIVE	SHORT ANSWERS
am I?	Yes, I am./No, I'm not.
are you?	Yes, you are./No, you aren't.
is he?	Yes, he is./No, he isn't.
is she?	Yes, she is./No, she isn't.
is it?	Yes, it is./No, it isn't.

Pronouns
he she

Articles
a + consonant
an + vowel

Question word
How?

Possessive adjectives
my your his
her its

Possessive *'s*
Rosie*'s* brother

Preposition
in London

See the Grammar Reference section at the back of the book for more information.

3 Meeting people

Greetings

Focus

- Personal relationships
- Social behaviour
- Family members

- Further practice: greeting, introducing, thanking, leaving

- Verb *to be* (plural): *are*
- Question: *Who?*

1 Listen and read. Are these sentences true or false?

1 James and Rosie are strangers.
2 James and Maria are friends.
3 Rosie and Alan are friends.
4 James and Alan are strangers.
5 Julia and Linda are friends.
6 Linda and Don are strangers.

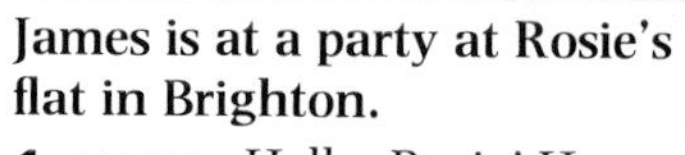

James is at a party at Rosie's flat in Brighton.

1 JAMES: Hello, Rosie! How are you?
ROSIE: Hi, James! I'm fine. How are you?

2 JAMES: Hello. I'm James Brady. What's your name?
MARIA: Hello. I'm Maria Cabral. Nice to meet you, James.

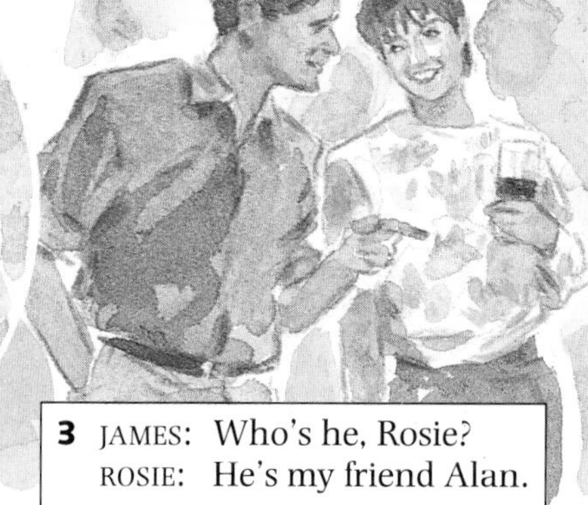

3 JAMES: Who's he, Rosie?
ROSIE: He's my friend Alan.

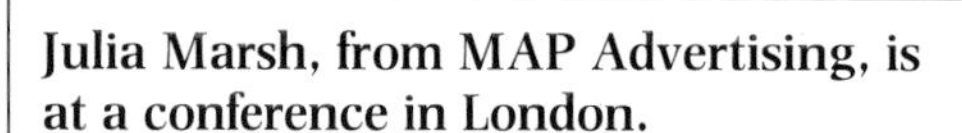

Julia Marsh, from MAP Advertising, is at a conference in London.

4 JULIA: Hello, Linda. How are you?
LINDA: I'm fine, thanks. How are you?
JULIA: I'm very well, thank you.

5 JULIA: Linda, this is Don Baker. Don, this is Linda White.
LINDA: How do you do.
DON: How do you do.

2 **Stress and intonation. Listen and repeat.**

Hello. Hello, Rosie! Hi.

How are you? How do you do.

Nice to meet you.

3 **Match the pictures with these expressions.**

Picture 1 – Hi!

Good morning, madam. Hi! How do you do.
Bye! Good afternoon. Good evening, sir.

4 **Talk about the people in the pictures above.**

The people in Picture ... are friends.
The people in Picture ... are strangers.

COMPARING CULTURES

5 **Read what Tom Hall does when he meets people. Say who is with Tom in each picture.**

A: *Picture 1. Who's she?*
B: *I think she's his mother.*

"I hug my sister when I meet her, but not my brother – I shake hands with my brother. I kiss my mother, my wife, and my children. I shake hands with strangers, but not with friends."

Now tell the class what you do when you meet someone.

6 **Complete the chart with expressions in English for meeting and leaving people.**

	MEETING	LEAVING
Friends/family	*Hello, ...*	....., ...
Others	....., ...	....., ...

Do you use different expressions in your language for different people?

Identities

Focus

- Further practice: family members, personal relationships
- Pronouns: *we, they*
- Possessive adjectives: *our, their*
- Possessive *s'*
- Adverb: *here*
- Plurals: + *es*, + *ies*, *men, women, children, people*
- Prepositions: *to* + country, *in* + street
- Further practice: verb *to be* (plural): *are ('re)*
- Zero article: *they're managers*

1 Listen to some conversations from Rosie's party. Complete the chart.

	NATIONALITY	JOB
James	*Irish*	*account manager*
Maria	.....	.....
Alan	.....	.....
Rosie	.....	.....

2 Now check that you have the correct information. Ask your partner.

A: *Is Maria a doctor?*
B: *No, she isn't.*

DISCOVERING LANGUAGE

3 Look at the pictures of Tom and Amanda. When do we use *they*?

He's a manager. **She's** a manager.
They're/are managers.

4 Now talk about these people's jobs.

Teresa and Marco (student)
They're students.

1 Rosie and Alan (nurse)
2 Peter (builder)
3 Jenny and Steve (musician)
4 Jason (painter)
5 Krystyna and Sara (doctor)
6 Suzy (shop assistant)

5 Look at the photographs of Graziella and the Gay family. Then read about them and answer the questions.

Graziella's from Switzerland, but she's in Britain now. She's a student of English.

Pauline and Sean Gay are British. They're married with two daughters. Their daughters' names are Hannah and Ella. Graziella is a guest in their house. The house is in south London.

Pauline and Sean/Irish?
A: *Are Pauline and Sean Irish?*
B: *No, they aren't.*

Pauline and Sean/British?
A: *Are Pauline and Sean British?*
B: *Yes, they are.*

1 Pauline and Sean/French?
2 Pauline and Sean/married?
3 Ella and Hannah/sisters?
4 Ella and Hannah/Pauline's daughters?
5 Ella and Hannah/Graziella's sisters?

6 Complete the sentences with *they, their, she* and *her*.

1 Graziella is a visitor to Britain. ..... is Swiss. ..... mother and father are in Switzerland now. ..... are in Ticino.
2 Pauline and Sean are married. ..... house is in London. Hannah and Ella are ..... daughters.

DISCOVERING LANGUAGE

7 Look at these two sentences.

1 Their guest's name is Graziella.
2 Their daughters' names are Hannah and Ella.

How many guests are there in sentence 1? How many daughters are there in sentence 2? What is the rule for possessive *'s* and *s'*?

8 Now add *'s* or *s'* to the sentences.

That's my friend house. (Kate and John)
That's my friends' house.
That's my friend house. (Rosie)
That's my friend's house.

1 That's my friend guitar. (Joe)
2 My sister telephone number is 42344. (Susan and Catherine)
3 My friend cassettes are here. (Paula and Tom)
4 My brother school is in London. (Mark)

9 Sean Gay is talking to Graziella. Read what he says.

" This is a map of London. We are here, in Earlsfield. Our house is here. Your school is here, in Oxford Street. "

10 Work in pairs. You don't know where you are in London.

Student A: Look at the map of central London. Ask your partner about numbers 1, 3 and 5. Then answer your partner's questions about numbers 2, 4 and 6.
Student B: Turn to page 117. Answer and then ask.

A: *Number one. Where are we?*
B: *We're in Regent Street.*

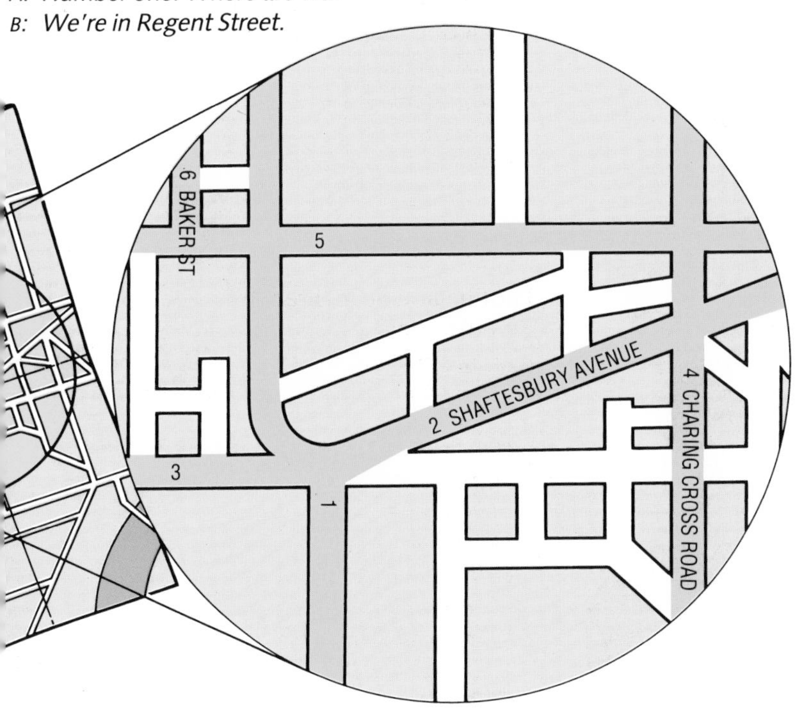

11 Work with a partner. Write sentences that are true for both of you using *we* and *our*.

We're in Milan. Our teacher is Mrs Luca.

DISCOVERING LANGUAGE

12 Look at these singular and plural nouns. What are the rules for making plurals with *es* and *ies*?

SINGULAR	PLURAL
shop	shop**s**
class	class**es**
country	countr**ies**
diary	diar**ies**
boss	boss**es**

Now note these irregular plural forms:

SINGULAR	PLURAL
man	**men**
woman	**women**
child	**children**
person	**people**

13 Pronunciation. Say the plural forms of these words. Then listen and repeat.

teacher steak secretary
cassette glass café

14 Listen. Do these words end in the sound /s/, /z/ or /ɪz/? Put them in the correct group.

mechanics nurses computers
friends addresses books
cafés nationalities students
numbers

1 /s/ shops *mechanics*
2 /z/ hamburgers *computers*
3 /ɪz/ classes *nurses*

Numbers

Focus

- Numbers 11–100
- Age
- Colours
- Further practice: personal information

- Asking someone to repeat something

- Questions: *How old?*, *What colour?*
- Further practice: verb *to be* (plural)

1 Say these numbers. Then spell them.

a) 6 b) 2 c) 10 d) 4 e) 1
f) 8 g) 3 h) 7 i) 9 j) 5

2 Listen and repeat the numbers.

NUMBERS 11–100	
11 eleven	21 twenty-one
12 twelve	22 twenty-two
13 thirteen	30 thirty
14 fourteen	40 forty
15 fifteen	50 fifty
16 sixteen	60 sixty
17 seventeen	70 seventy
18 eighteen	80 eighty
19 nineteen	90 ninety
20 twenty	100 a hundred

Now listen and repeat the pairs of numbers.

13 thirteen 30 thirty

3 Work in pairs. Your partner is one of the people below. Ask about his/her age. Guess who he/she is.

A: *How old are you?*
B: *I'm twenty-five.*
A: *Are you James?*
B: *Yes, I am.*

4 Ask and answer about people in your class.

A: *How old are you?*
B: *I'm nineteen.*
A: *How old is Juan?*
B: *He's eighteen./I don't know.*

5 Look at the pictures of people in this unit. Ask and answer.

A: *Who's he?*
B: *He's . . .*
A: *How old is he?*
B: *He's . . .*

A: *Who are they?*
B: *They're . . . and . . .*
A: *How old are they?*
B: *I think they're . . .*

6 Rosie keeps a note of important numbers on her computer. Listen and write the numbers on the chart below.

PERSONAL INFORMATION	
Name	*Rosie Brady*
Address	..... *Egremont Road*
Telephone	.....
Passport	.....
Driving licence	.....
Bank account	.....
Other	.....

7 Ask and answer about the numbers.

A: *What's Rosie's house number?*
B: *Thirty-seven.*
A: *What's her telephone number?*
B: *Three double two nine four.*

8 Now ask your partner.

A: *What's your passport number?*
B: *345012.*

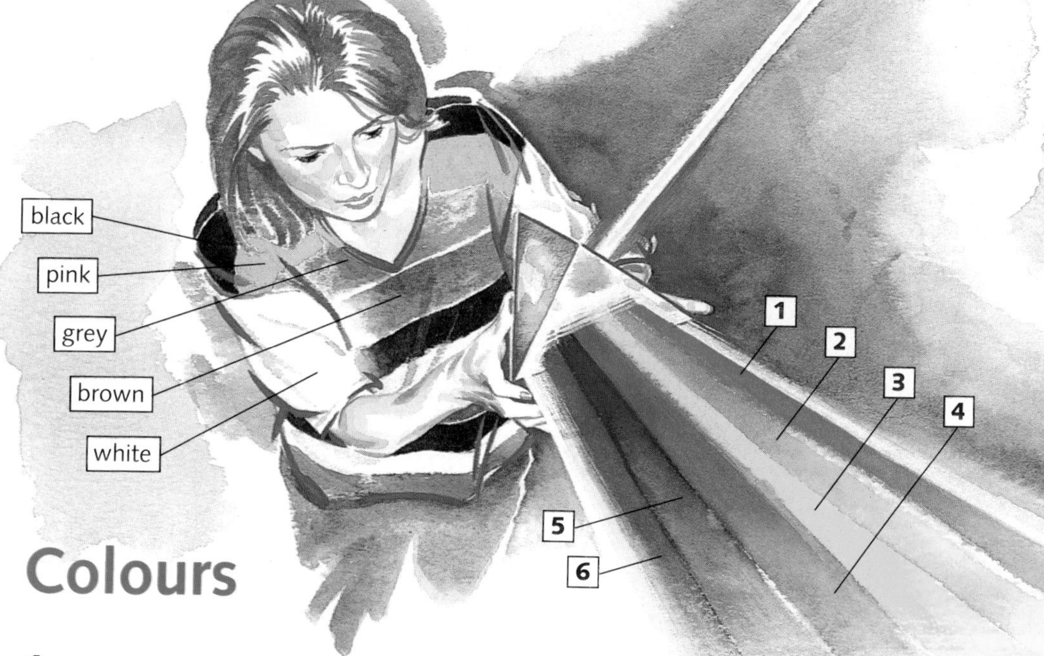

Colours

1 Listen. Match the numbered colours in the picture with the names of the colours below.

1 – red

orange blue black red white green brown purple yellow grey pink

2 Look at the objects in Exercise 6 on page 24. Ask and answer about colour.

A: *What colour's the telephone?*
B: *It's black.*

A: *What colour are the pencils?*
B: *They're brown.*

COMPARING CULTURES

3 Look at the pictures below. What colour are these things in Britain? What colour are they in your country? Write sentences.

passports
I think passports are red in Britain. They're blue in Turkey.

fire engines ambulances police cars post boxes

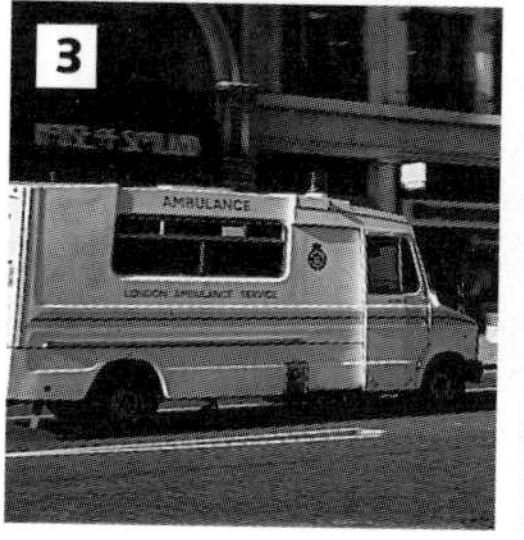

4 Pronunciation. Listen to the vowel sounds in the words.

1 /ɒ/ on, shop
2 /ɔː/ four, your
3 /ʊ/ book, look
4 /uː/ two, food
5 /ʌ/ bus, hug

Listen again and repeat. Then match the words below with the vowel sounds 1–5.

from – vowel 1

1 from 4 forty 7 blue
2 much 5 school 8 good
3 job 6 boss

Now listen and check your answers.

ENGLISH AROUND YOU

Development

LISTENING

1 Listen to the conversations and write the names of the people in each picture. Choose from the list below.

Picture 1 – Julia Marsh, Sandra Turner

Susan Warren   Paul Cook   James Brady
Julia Marsh   Tom Hall   Sandra Turner

2 Listen again. Do these people know each other (A), or are they strangers (B)?

Julia and Sandra – A

1 Sandra and Paul
2 Tom and Susan
3 Tom and Paul
4 Paul and Susan
5 Julia and James
6 James and Susan
7 James and Paul

3 Name two people who do *not* work for MAP Advertising.

4 Match the people with the jobs.

James Brady – Account Manager

1 James Brady	Managing Director (MAP)
2 Tom Hall	Receptionist (MAP)
3 Paul Cook	Account Manager (MAP)
4 Sandra Turner	Account Manager (MAP)
5 Julia Marsh	Marketing Manager (Brentwood Engineering)
6 Susan Warren	Designer (Art and Design Limited)

READING

5 Look at these things from Sandra's bag. Match them with things on the list below.

1 – video club cards

a telephone card theatre tickets train tickets
a credit card video club cards a library card

SPEAKING AND WRITING

6 Work in pairs.

Student A: Look at the objects above. Ask about colours, numbers and prices. Write the answers.
Student B: Turn to page 117. Answer your partner's questions.

A: *What colour is the library card? What number is it? What colour are ... ? What price is/are ... ?*
B: *It's ...*

WRITING: A list

7 Work in pairs.

Student A: Tell your partner about the cards and tickets in your bag or pockets.
Student B: Write a list of your partner's objects, with colours, numbers and prices.

Two white bus tickets, numbers 15346 and 43259, prices four francs and nine francs.

Summary

FUNCTIONAL LANGUAGE

Greeting someone
Hello. How are you?
Hi. I'm fine/very well, thanks.
Good morning/afternoon/evening.
How do you do.
Nice to meet you.

Leaving someone
Bye!

Asking someone to repeat something
Can you say that again, please?

Asking about people
Who's he?
He's my friend.
Who are they?
They're my friends.

Asking someone's age
How old are you?
I'm twenty-five.

Using numbers
eleven-a hundred

Asking about colour
What colour is it?
It's grey.
What colour are they?
They're red.

GRAMMAR

The verb *to be*: the present simple tense – plural

AFFIRMATIVE		NEGATIVE	
FULL FORM	SHORT FORM	FULL FORM	SHORT FORM
we are	we're	we are not	we aren't
you are	you're	you are not	you aren't
they are	they're	they are not	they aren't

INTERROGATIVE	SHORT ANSWERS
are we?	Yes, we are./No, we aren't.
are you?	Yes, you are./No, you aren't.
are they ?	Yes, they are./No, they aren't.

Pronouns
we they

Zero article
They're managers.

Plurals with *es* and *ies*
class classes
secretary secretaries

Irregular plural forms
man men
woman women
child children
person people

Question words
Who? How old?
What colour?
What price?

Prepositions
to Britain
in Oxford Street

Possessive adjectives
our their

Possessive *s'*
my parents' house

Adverb
here

See the Grammar Reference section at the back of the book for more information.

Progress check 1

Vocabulary

1 Change the sentences. Write the nationality.

He's from Japan.
He's Japanese.

1 She's from Britain.
2 I'm from Portugal.
3 We're from Spain.
4 They're from Brazil.
5 It's from France.
6 You're from Italy.

2 Label the colours on the flags.

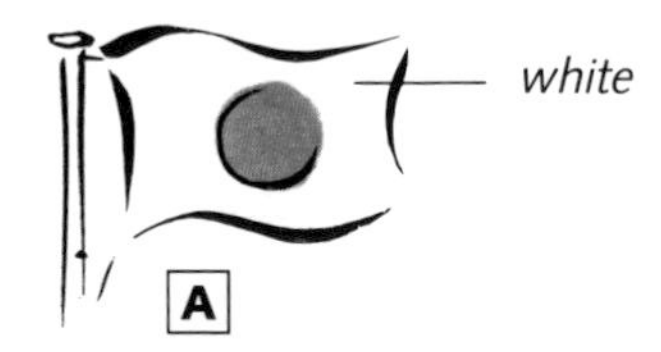

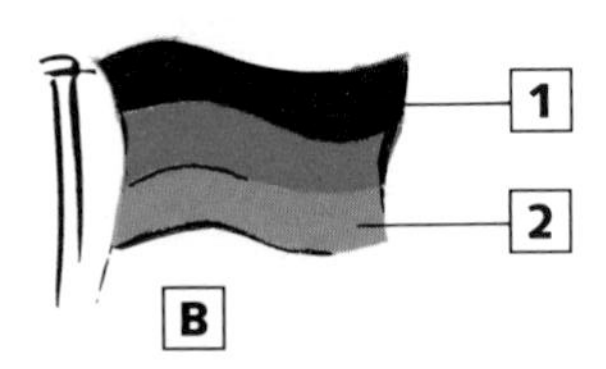

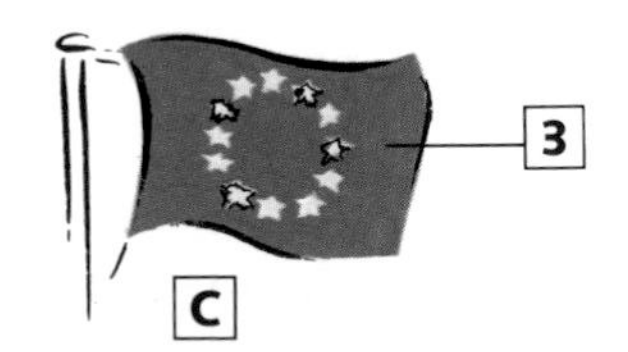

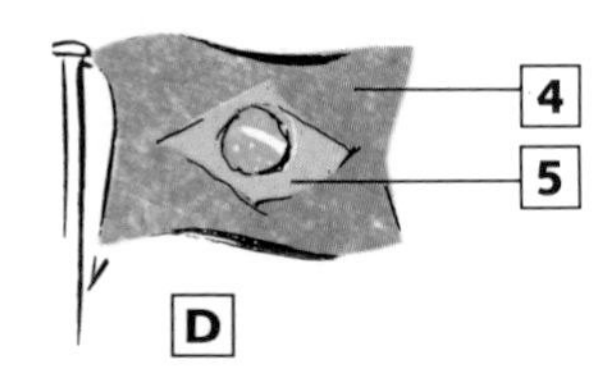

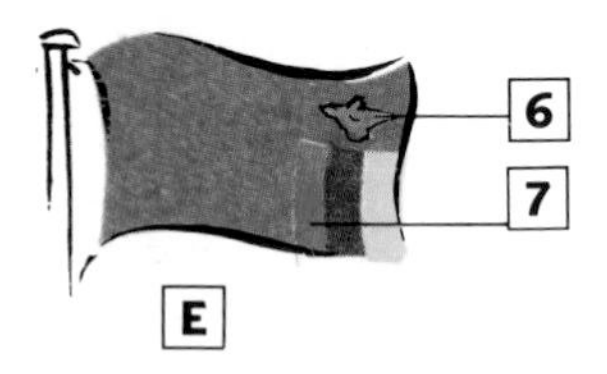

3 Write the people's jobs.

She's a teacher.

4 Write the numbers.

12 – *twelve*

a) 3 b) 15 c) 13 d) 50 e) 30 f) 100 g) 84 h) 22

Grammar and functions

5 Replace the words in italics with *he/she/they/his/her/their*.

James is from Ireland.
He is from Ireland.

1 *Rosie and Maria* are in Brighton.
2 *Tom's* company is MAP Advertising.
3 *James and Julia's* office is in London.
4 Is this *Pauline and Sean's* house?
5 Maria is *Rosie's* friend.
6 How old is *Alan*?
7 Who are *Susan and Paul*?
8 *Rosie* is a nurse.

6 Add *a/an* to the nouns.

school – *a school*

1 company
2 office
3 hospital
4 address
5 street
6 town
7 information desk
8 café
9 bank
10 airport
11 hotel
12 bus stop

7 Answer the questions. Use short answers.

Is Rome the capital of Italy?
Yes, it is.

1 Is Paris the capital of Spain?
2 Are Rosie and James American?
3 Is Hollywood in the United States?
4 Is Tom Hall from Ireland?
5 Are you a student?
6 Are you British?

8 **Write the plural form of these nouns.**

class – *classes*

1 child	4 book	7 salary
2 nationality	5 telephone	8 address
3 woman	6 person	9 doctor

9 **Complete the sentences with *in*, *to* or *from*.**

1 Marco's Italian. He's ..... Rome.
2 Rome is ..... Italy.
3 James's hotel is ..... Maysoule Street.
4 What's 'hotel' ..... Italian?
5 Maria is a visitor ..... Britain.
6 Teresa is ..... London now.

10 **Complete the conversation.**

MAN: What's your name, please?
WOMAN: Ellis. Karen Ellis.
MAN: (1) ..... ?
WOMAN: E-L-L-I-S.
MAN: Thank you. (2) ..... address?
WOMAN: 23 Gilbert Road, here in Brighton.
MAN: Right. And (3) ..... ?
WOMAN: 64116.
MAN: And (4) ..... ?
WOMAN: The United States. I'm from Chicago.
MAN: OK. (5) ..... ?
WOMAN: I'm twenty-one.
MAN: And (6) ..... ?
WOMAN: No, I'm single.

11 **Address an envelope to Karen.**

12 **Read the paragraph about Karen. Then write a paragraph about yourself. Give the same information.**

Her name's Karen. She's twenty-one and she's single. She's American. She's from Chicago.

My name's ...

13 **Write a question for each answer.**

It's a computer.
What is it?

1 It's grey.
2 It's in a shop.
3 Japan.
4 £399.

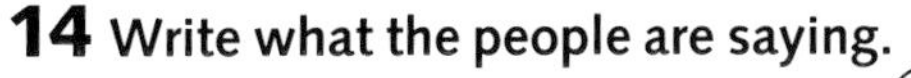

14 **Write what the people are saying.**

Common errors

15 **Add one word to correct each sentence.**

What your name?
What is your name?

1 My name Yoshiko.
2 Where you from?
3 I Spanish.
4 The bank? Is there.
5 I am musician.

16 **Correct the word order.**

How you are?
How are you?

1 How much it is?
2 How old you are?
3 They are married or single?
4 Where he is from?
5 What does mean 'envelope'?

17 **Correct the spelling of the words in bold print.**

There from Brazil.
They're from Brazil.

1 Where are **there** bags?
2 Our books are **their**.
3 She's **they're** doctor.
4 **Their** American computers.
5 **Its** my passport.
6 Where's the hotel? What's **it's** address?

At the end of the Progress Check, look back at your mistakes and study the Grammar Reference section if you need more help.

4 Food and drink

MAYFLOWER RESTAURANT

BILL

Soup (2)	£2.95
Steak	£13.00
Chicken	£10.20
Coffee	£1.25
Orange juice	£1.65
TOTAL:	£26.35

Thank you for your custom. Please call again.

In a restaurant

Focus

- Food and drink (in a restaurant)
- Dishes in different countries
- Ingredients
- Further practice: money
- Further practice: asking for something, asking prices
- *Can I have ... ?*
- *Would like* + infinitive
- Zero article: *(I'd like) steak and chips*
- Question: *Which?*
- Further practice: *I'd like*, question: *How much?*

1 Look at the menu. Which words for food and drink are the same in your language? Which words are nearly the same?

2 Ask and answer about prices.

A: *How much is the tea?*
B: *Ninety pence/Ninety p. (90p)*
A: *How much is the spaghetti?*
B: *Seven pounds seventy-five. (£7.75)*
A: *How much are the pancakes?*
B: *Three pounds forty-five. (£3.45)*

3 Listen and read. Write what Tom and James want to eat and drink.

Tom – Food: soup, ... Drink: ...

TOM: Excuse me. Can I have the menu, please?
WAITRESS: Oh ... yes, sir.
TOM: Thank you.

Later ...

WAITRESS: Yes, sir.
TOM: Soup, please.
WAITRESS: Soup.
TOM: And I'd like steak, chips, and salad, please. James?
JAMES: I'd like soup ... and chicken, please.
WAITRESS: Thank you. What would you like to drink?
TOM: A bottle of mineral water, please.
JAMES: And a glass of apple juice for me, please.

MAYFLOWER RESTAURAN

MENU

STARTERS

Prawn cocktail £4.50
French onion soup £2.95

MAIN COURSES

Fried chicken £9.50
Roast lamb £10.20
Spaghetti bolognese £7.75
Steak £13.00
Fish of the day £11.3
Hamburger £6.25

All main courses served with chips and fresh vegetables or mixed salad.

DESSERTS

American pancakes £3.45
Fresh fruit salad £3.25
Strawberry cake £4.50
Ice cream £3.90
Cheese and biscuits £3.95

DRINKS

Mineral water £1.50 Tea 90p Coffee £1.2
Fruit juice (orange, apple, grapefruit) £1.85

All prices include VAT · Service not included

4 Look at the menu again and check the bill. There are some mistakes in the bill. Write it correctly.

5 Stress and intonation. Listen and repeat.

I'd like chicken, chips and salad, please.

Now ask for:

1 soup, a hamburger and coffee
2 soup, spaghetti and salad

6 Work in pairs. Use the example to help you start the conversation.

Student A: You are a customer. Ask for the menu. Order food and drink. Ask for the bill.
Student B: You are a waiter/waitress.

A: *Excuse me. Can I have the menu, please?*
B: *Yes, sir/madam.*
B: *What would you like to eat/drink?*
A: *I'd like chicken, please.*
B: *Certainly, madam/sir.*

Food around the world

COMPARING CULTURES

1 Look at the different dishes in the pictures. Match the dishes with the countries below.

1 – Italy

India   Italy   the United States   Mexico   Spain   Morocco   Japan

2 Ask and answer about each dish. Follow this example:

A: *Picture 1. What's it called?*
B: *It's a pizza.*
A: *Which country is it from?*
B: *It's from Italy.*
A: *What are the ingredients?*
B: *Flour, cheese, tomatoes, mushrooms and oil.*

3 Make lists of all the ingredients in the pictures.

MEAT	VEGETABLES
beef, ...	tomato, ...
FRUIT	**OTHER**
...	flour, ...

4 Add these words to your lists. Check your dictionary.

cabbage   banana   bread
yoghurt   sausage   grape
pear   orange   bean   apple
turkey   grapefruit   fish   pea
noodles   chicken

beef   bread   carrot   cauliflower   cheese   couscous
egg   lamb   lettuce   mushroom   onion   pepper
potato   prawn   rice   seaweed   tomato

Pancakes

INGREDIENTS
200g flour
2 eggs
500ml milk
40g butter

TO SERVE
sugar
1 lemon

Focus

- Containers for food
- Weights of food
- Further practice: ingredients

- Further practice: buying things

- Countables/ uncountables
- Determiners: *some/any*
- *There is/There are*
- Irregular plural: *loaves*
- Prepositions: *in* (the cupboard), *on* (the table)
- Further practice: *I'd like ...*

Preparing food

1 Rosie and Alan are making pancakes. Look at the ingredients above. Listen and complete the conversation with *a(n), some* or *any*.

ROSIE: OK. Two hundred grams of flour.
ALAN: Yes. There's (1) ..... flour in the cupboard.
ROSIE: Are there (2) ..... eggs?
ALAN: Yes. I think there are (3) ..... eggs in the fridge.
ROSIE: Is there (4) ..... lemon there too?
ALAN: There aren't (5) ..... lemons. Oh, sorry, there is one.
ROSIE: OK. There's (6) ..... milk and (7) ..... butter in the fridge too.
ALAN: Right. Oh no! There isn't (8) ..... sugar!
ROSIE: Yes, there is. It's on the table.

Check your answers with your partner. Then practise the conversation.

DISCOVERING LANGUAGE

2 Look at these nouns from the conversation. Which are countable, and which are uncountable?

flour egg lemon
milk butter sugar

3 Now complete the chart with *a(n), some* or *any*.

	COUNTABLE NOUNS		UNCOUNTABLE NOUNS
	Singular	Plural	
Affirmative	a (lemon)	some (eggs)	some (sugar)
Negative	a (lemon)	.....	.....
Interrogative	a (lemon)	.....	.....

4 Look at the picture above. Look at the things on the table for one minute. Then close the book and make ten sentences about them. Begin: *There's a/some ..., There are some ..., There isn't a/any ..., There aren't any ...* .

There's some milk.

5 Work in pairs.

Student A: Look at the picture above. How many differences are there between your picture and your partner's picture? Ask and answer.

Student B: Turn to page 117. Answer and ask.

A: *In your picture, is there any milk on the table?*
B: *Yes, there is. In your picture, are there any pears in the bowl?*
A: *No, there aren't.*

6 **Look at these words for talking about food and drink.**

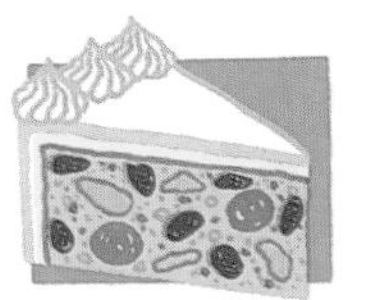
a **piece** of cake

a **packet** of sugar

a **bottle** of oil

a **tin** of peas

a **pound** (= about 450 grams) of cheese

five **pounds** (= about 2.25 kilos) of potatoes

a **loaf** of bread (two **loaves**)

a **bunch** of grapes

7 **Pronunciation. Listen to the sound /ə/ in the underlined parts of the phrases.**

a piece of cake	a bottle of oil	a bunch of grapes
a packet of sugar	a tin of peas	a glass of milk
a pound of cheese	a loaf of bread	a cup of tea

Listen again and repeat.

8 **Think of a dish from your country. Make a list of all the ingredients. Then write how much you want to buy of each ingredient. Keep the list for Exercise 10.**

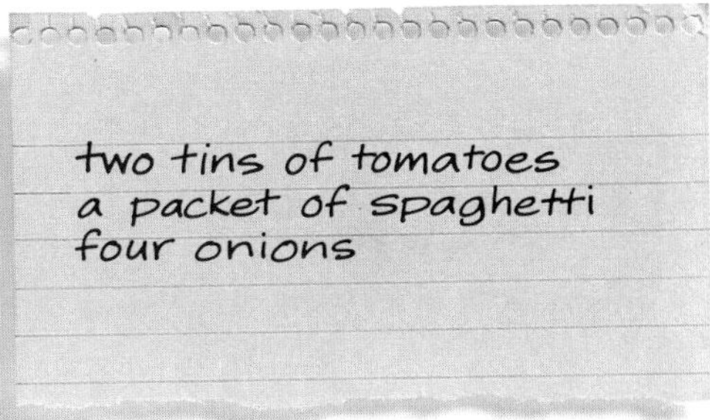

two tins of tomatoes
a packet of spaghetti
four onions

9 **Listen to two conversations in a shop and list what the people buy.**

CONVERSATION 1 six eggs, ...
CONVERSATION 2 ....

Listen again to Conversation 2 and answer the questions .

The shop assistant asks, 'Can I help you?'

1 What is the customer's answer?
2 What are the customer's words when she gives her money to the shop assistant?

10 **Work in pairs.**

Student A: Look at your list from Exercise 8. Buy the food on it from your partner's shop.
Student B: You are a shop assistant. Turn to page 118.

A: *I'd like ... Can I have ... ?*
B: *There's some ... /I'm sorry, there isn't any ...*

Now change roles.

ENGLISH AROUND YOU

Development

11AM TO 2PM
COMPLETE
Pasta Dinners
$2.85
Regular or Hot
JUMBO TORPEDO ROLL
SANDWICHES
Choice of: CAPICOLLO • SAUSAGE • MEATBALL • ITALIAN BEEF • SALAMI • CORNED BEEF • PASTRAMI • MORTADELLA • HAM • TURKEY OR VEGGIE
2.75
EACH PLUS TAX
PARTY SANDWICHES
3 and 5 feet
$11.00 a foot
BUON GIORNO

SPEAKING

1 Look at the pictures and the signs. Say what you think.

1 Is this a restaurant?
2 Which country is the food from?
3 Name some things that people can buy here.

READING

2 Read the extract on the right from a guide to restaurants and food shops and check your answers to Exercise 1.

3 Read the extract and look at the signs again.

1 What would you like to buy at Buon Giorno? Choose:
- something hot
- something cold

I'd like a turkey sandwich.

2 How much is the big party sandwich?

14 EATING GUIDE · ST PAUL, MINNESOTA

A TASTE OF ITA

BUON GIORNO ITALIAN MARKET
335 UNIVERSITY AVENUE, ST PAUL

Frank MacKondy is the manager of this friendly takeaway food shop. He sells home-made hot and cold Italian food: soup, pizza, pasta dishes and salads. He also sells differe kinds of sandwiches; for example, chicken, turkey, salami, beef, cheese and egg. These are served hot or cold, too.

Frank's party sandwiches are a speciality. One sandwich is big enough for thirty people!

BRITISH FARE

FISH AND CHIPS · 2055 RIVER DRIVE, ST PAUL

LISTENING

4 Frank is talking to three customers. Listen and complete the chart with the food and drink each customer wants. Choose from this list.

turkey sandwich potato chicken sandwich beef sandwich salami cheese tomato egg sandwich lettuce salad soup spaghetti chips rice cream white coffee black coffee tea apple juice mayonnaise French dressing tomato sauce oil

	FOOD	DRINK
Customer 1	*chicken sandwich, ...*	.....
Customer 2	....., ...	______
Customer 3	....., ...	.....

SPEAKING: Roleplay

5 Work in pairs.

Student A: You are Frank. Ask what your customer wants to eat and drink.
Student B: You are a customer. Ask Frank for some food and drink.

WRITING: A fax

6 You can order food at Buon Giorno by fax. Look at the example. Then write a fax to Buon Giorno. Ask for the food you want.

FAX TRANSMISSION

To: Buon Giorno Italian Market
From: John Dayton
Date: June 27th **Sheets:** 1

MESSAGE

I'd like two beef and cheese sandwiches, one vegetable soup and two cups of black coffee. Please deliver the food to: 702 Washington Avenue. Thank you.

John Dayton

WRITING: Punctuation

7 Capital letters are used for names and at the beginning of sentences. Rewrite the paragraph correctly.

frank's shop is called buon giorno italian market. it's in st paul, minnesota, near the centre of town. frank's sandwiches and hot food are very popular.

Summary

FUNCTIONAL LANGUAGE

Asking what someone wants
What would you like to eat?
Can I help you?

Asking about food
What's it called?
Which country is it from?
What are the ingredients?

Talking about prices
How much is the tea?
Ninety pence/Ninety p.
One pound twenty-five.

Describing what there is/isn't
There's an apple in the cupboard.
Is there a banana in the cupboard?
There aren't any lemons in the fridge.

Asking for something
Can I have the menu, please?
I'd like chicken/some chicken, please.

GRAMMAR

Countable nouns

SINGULAR	PLURAL
a tomato	tomatoes
a tin of soup	tins of soup

Uncountable nouns
cream
spaghetti

Some/any

	+ PLURAL NOUNS	+ UNCOUNTABLE NOUNS
AFFIRMATIVE	There are *some* lemons.	There's *some* orange juice.
NEGATIVE	There aren't *any* eggs.	There isn't *any* chicken.
INTERROGATIVE	Are there *any* sandwiches?	Is there *any* milk?

There is/there are

	SINGULAR	PLURAL
AFFIRMATIVE	there is	there are
NEGATIVE	there isn't	there aren't
INTERROGATIVE	is there?	are there ?
SHORT ANSWERS	Yes, there is. No, there isn't.	Yes, there are. No, there aren't.

Zero article
I'd like steak and chips.

Irregular plural forms
loaf loaves
foot feet

Question word
Which?

Modal: *can*
Can I have ... ?

***Would like* + infinitive**
What would you like to eat?

Prepositions
in the cupboard
on the table

See the Grammar Reference section at the back of the book for more information.

5 A place to live

A new home

Focus

- Places to live
- Rooms
- Facilities

- Verb: *have got*
- Prepositions: *next to, between, near, opposite, on* (the ground floor)
- Question: *How many?*
- Conjunction: *because*
- *He'd like ...*
- Further practice: *there is/are*

Marine Drive, Brighton
Tel: (0273) 64211
Fax: (0273) 64205

▼ Coffee bar

▼ Comfortable sitting roo

Eldon House is a hostel for international students. It is in the centre of Brighton, near the sea and ten minutes' walk from the station.

The hostel has got very good facilities. There are twenty single bedrooms on three floors, with a bathroom and a kitchen on each floor. A small number of double bedrooms with private bathrooms are also available.

▲ Games room
▼ Single bedroo

▲ Kitchen on each floor

▼ Large dining room

On the ground floor there is a large sitting room with a television and a telephone. There is also a small coffee bar and a games room with a billiard table and table tennis-table.

For more information, please contact the manager, Mr Alex Langton.

1 **Read the brochure opposite about the student hostel where Rosie's friend Maria lives. Answer the questions.**

1 Where is Eldon House?
2 How many single bedrooms are there?
3 How many kitchens are there?
4 Where is the television?
5 Where is the table-tennis table?

2 **Listen and read. Maria is talking to Rosie. Match the numbers on the plan with the rooms.**

Jane	1	Sally	kitchen	shop
Sara	Maria	Eva		2
dining room				3 ☎

1 – bathroom

ROSIE: How's your hostel, Maria?
MARIA: Great! I've got a big bedroom.
ROSIE: Has it got a bathroom?
MARIA: No, it hasn't, but there's a bathroom opposite my room, between Jane's room and Sally's room.
ROSIE: Aha. Is there a nice sitting room?
MARIA: Yes, there is. It's big and it's got a television and a telephone.
ROSIE: Is there a coffee bar?
MARIA: Yes – there's a small one next to the sitting room.
ROSIE: What about a garden?
MARIA: No, there isn't a garden. But it's near the sea.
ROSIE: Oh, it sounds very nice.

3 **Describe to your partner where the ground-floor rooms are in Eldon House. Use the words below.**

Maria's room is next to Sara's room.

next to between near opposite

4 **James is talking to Rosie. Listen and note which facilities there are in his hotel.**

restaurant, ...

5 **Ask and answer about the facilities in the hotel and in the bedrooms.**

A: *Has the hotel got a coffee bar?*
B: *Yes, it has./No, it hasn't.*

A: *Have the rooms got radios?*
B: *Yes, they have./No, they haven't.*

6 **Now write about James's hotel. What's it called? Where is it? What facilities has it got? There is more information about it in Unit 2.**

7 **James would like to live in a flat. Listen and note the answers to these questions:**

1 What would he like in his flat?
2 Where would he like to live?

8 **Read the advertisements. Say which flat you think he'd like. Say why.**

I think he'd like the flat in ... because it's got ...

HOUSES & FLATS TO LET

FLAT – WINDSOR Large two-bedroom flat on the ground floor of a modern development. Small garden. London 40 minutes by train. Telephone 0753 92214 after 6.30 p.m.

FLAT – PADDINGTON, LONDON W2 One-bedroom flat near shops and station. Fourth floor. Large sitting room, kitchen, bathroom Tel: 071 724 66519 evenings.

FLAT – WIMBLEDON, LONDON SW19 Bedroom, sitting room, small kitchen and bathroom, large garden. Good bus and train services to central London. Tel: 071-580 94672 (day) 081-946 37441 (evening).

9 **James has got a flat now. Write the questions that you think Rosie asks.**

JAMES: I've got a flat!
ROSIE: Oh, good. (1) ..... ?
JAMES: In South London.
ROSIE: (2) ..... ?
JAMES: Yes, it has. A large one.
ROSIE: Great! (3) ..... ?
JAMES: A hundred and fifty pounds a week. That's OK.

Now listen and check your questions.

ENGLISH AROUND YOU

Possessions

Focus

- Possessions
- People's lives (home, work, leisure)
- Further practice: places to live

- Present simple tense: affirmative (singular)
- Prepositions: *in* (a flat), *at* (weekends)
- Further practice: verb: *have got*, determiners: *some, any*

1 Work in pairs. Rosie's boyfriend, Alan, is moving to a new house.

Student A: Look at the picture. Guess what Alan's got.

Student B: Turn to page 118. Say if your partner is correct.

A: *He's got a ...*
He's got some ...
Has he got a ... ?
Has he got any ... ?
B: *Yes, he has./No, he hasn't.*

2 Ask and answer.

A: *What have you got on your desk/in your bag/in your pockets?*
B: *I've got ...*
A: *How many ... have you got?*
B: *I've got (three).*

COMPARING CULTURES

3 Most varieties of English are very similar, but we sometimes use different words or structures in different countries.

What are the differences? Are there differences in your language in different regions or countries? Tell the class about some of them.

4 Stress and intonation. Listen and repeat.

Have you got a pen?

Have you got any money?

Yes, I have. No, I haven't.

5 Ask about your partner's house or flat. Note the answers.

A: *Have you got a/any ... ?*
B: *Yes, I/we have./No, I/we haven't.*
A: *Is there a ... ? Are there any ... ?*
Where's ... ? Where are ... ?

6 Now describe your partner's house or flat to the class.

Home, work and leisure

1 Read what Julia says.

"I live in a flat in London. I work at MAP Advertising. I study German at a language school after work. I play the piano in jazz clubs at weekends."

2 Talk about Julia.

*Julia live**s** in a flat in London.*
*She work**s** ... She stud**ies** ...*
*She play**s** ...*

DISCOVERING LANGUAGE

3 Look at the present simple tense verbs in Exercises 1 and 2 and complete the chart.

PRESENT SIMPLE TENSE: AFFIRMATIVE		
	's' ending? (yes/no)	Example
I/you	.....	.....
he/she/it	.....	.....

4 Talk about these people. Use the information in the pictures.

Maria lives ...

5 Write about two of the people above. Use the information about Julia in Exercises 1 and 2 to help you.

6 Now write about someone you know.

Rooms around the world

COMPARING CULTURES

1 Look at these pictures of sitting rooms in different countries. Which countries do you think they are in?

I think Number 1 is in ...

the United States   Morocco
Britain   Japan

Focus

- Furniture
- Living habits
- Further practice: colours

- Further practice: *have got, there is/there are*, present simple affirmative prepositions: *opposite, next to, between, on*

2 Find examples of the things below in Pictures 1–4. Use a dictionary to help you.

There's a clock in Picture 4.
There are some cushions in every picture.

fireplace door cushion plant light
coffee table clock mat floor flower
chair carpet wall picture lamp sofa
curtain window dining table shelf

3 **Now match these texts with the pictures.**

1 I sit here with my family in the evenings. We haven't got a television, so we talk and read books. We eat in another room.

2 I talk, eat and drink tea in this room with my family and friends. Sometimes I sleep here in the afternoons.

3 This is our sitting room, but we also eat and cook here. The dining table is in one part of the room and there is a small kitchen area in another part.

4 This is our sitting room, but we also eat and sleep here. We haven't got much furniture in the room, but there is a television.

4 **Read about Rosie's sitting room and then write about your sitting room.**

It's a big room. It's got white walls and green curtains. There are some bookshelves for books and plants, two sofas and an armchair. There are some pictures on the wall and there's a big fireplace.

5 **Now read about Rosie's bedroom. Copy the plan and draw the furniture in the correct place. Label the furniture.**

I like my bedroom. It's got a big white cupboard opposite the door, and next to
3 that is a desk with my computer on it. Between the desk and the window are
5 some shelves. They're black.
My bedroom's got white walls and
7 blue curtains. There's a lamp on a small table next to my bed.

6 **Read the text above again. What do these pronouns refer to?**

I (line 1) – *Rosie*

1 It (line 1) 2 it (line 3) 3 They (line 5)

7 **Work in pairs. Look at the furniture in the rooms below.**

Student A: Describe the kitchen in your house. Say what there is in it and where each thing is is.
Student B: Draw a plan of your partner's kitchen.
Student B: Describe the bathroom in your house. Say what there is in it and where each thing is.
Student A: Draw a plan of your partner's bathroom.

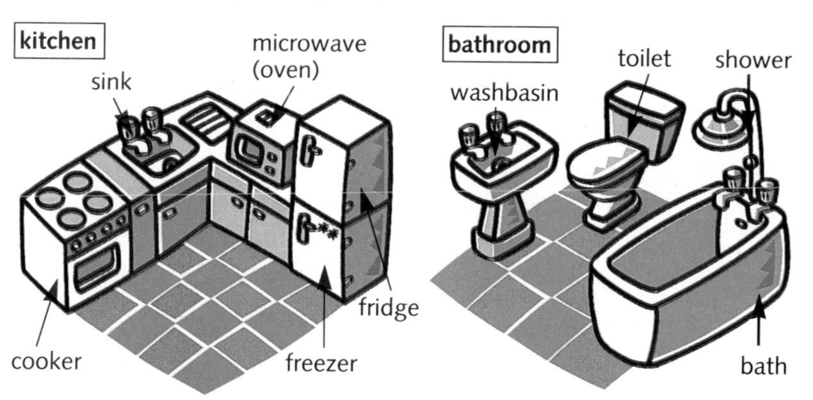

8 **Complete the chart with words from this unit and other words you know.**

FURNITURE YOU CAN SIT ON	*chair, . . .*
ELECTRICAL THINGS	*computer, . . .*
OTHER THINGS FOR A ROOM	*picture, . . .*
PARTS OF A ROOM (NOT FURNITURE)	*door, . . .*

9 **Pronunciation. Listen to the sound /tʃ/ in these words.**

chair chips which

Listen again and repeat.

Now listen to the sound /ʃ/ in these words.

shelf shower wash

Listen again and repeat.

Now say these words. Then listen and repeat.

shop chicken cheese mushrooms fish

DISCOVERING LANGUAGE

10 **Look at these shop signs. Which one is correct? Why?**

Development

SPEAKING

1 Cordelia Roe lives on a houseboat on the River Cam in Cambridge. Look at the pictures. Describe the boat and where it is. Use these words to help you:

river bank trees roof deck flowers

LISTENING

2 Listen to Cordelia. She is talking about the boat. The name of the boat is *Castle Eden*. Answer the questions.

1 How old is the boat?
2 Who lives on the boat with Cordelia?
3 Is it more fun on the boat in summer or in winter?
4 Look at the plan. Write the size of the boat.
5 Label the rooms. Choose from this list:

bedroom dining room library games room
bathroom sitting room engine room

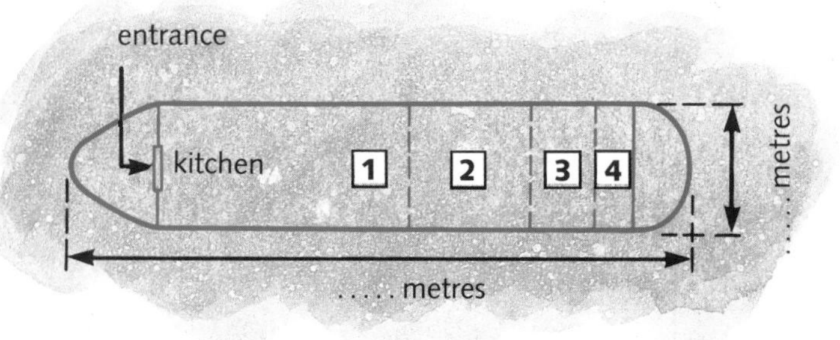

3 Listen again. List the furniture and equipment in two of these rooms: the kitchen, sitting room, bedroom, bathroom. Find students with the same lists and check your answers.

KITCHEN cooker, ...
SITTING ROOM stove, ...

4 Complete the text about Cordelia.

Cordelia Roe (1) ..... on a houseboat with (2) ..... husband Michael and two animals. Cordelia (3) ..... a nurse. She (4) ..... in Cambridge.

The boat (5) ..... small, but there (6) ..... five rooms, including the engine room. There (7) ..... a kitchen at the front of the boat. The boat (8) ..... also (9) ..... a bedroom, a bathroom and a sitting room. There (10) ..... electricity, so Cordelia and Michael (11) ..... a television and other electrical equipment. The boat is (12) ..... home.

READING

5 Read about houses in Britain and label Chart 1 with these phrases:

own homes council houses
private rented houses

Houses in Britain

There are about 23 million homes (houses and flats) in Britain. Sixteen million families live in their own homes. Five million people rent their homes from local councils and 2 million live in private rented houses.

A typical British house is for a family of two to four people. There are other houses next to it and opposite it, and there is a garden at the back and another at the front. A typical house has got two floors. On the ground floor there is a sitting room, a dining room and a kitchen. On the first floor, there's a bathroom and the bedrooms. Small houses have one or two bedrooms. Large houses have three or more.

Chart 1

....

Houses in Britain

Now complete Chart 2 below with information from the text.

Chart 2

A TYPICAL HOUSE	
Number of people	2–4
Garden? (Where?)	.....
Number of floors	.....
Number of ground-floor rooms	.....
Number of bedrooms	.....
Number of bathrooms	.....

WRITING: A paragraph

6 Complete a chart like Chart 2 above for a typical house or flat in your country. Then write a paragraph like Paragraph 2 in Exercise 5. Start like this:

A typical (Portuguese) house/flat is . . .

Summary

FUNCTIONAL LANGUAGE

Describing places to live
There's a large garden.
It's got two bedrooms.

Saying you do not understand
I'm sorry. I don't understand.

Talking about rates
A hundred and fifty pounds a week.

GRAMMAR

The verb *have got*: the present tense

AFFIRMATIVE

FULL FORM	SHORT FORM
I have got	I've got
you have got	you've got
he/she/it has got	he's/she's/it's got
we have got	we've got
they have got	they've got

NEGATIVE

FULL FORM	SHORT FORM
I have not got	I haven't got
you have not got	you haven't got
he/she/it has not got	he/she/it hasn't got
we have not got	we haven't got
they have not got	they haven't got

INTERROGATIVE	SHORT ANSWERS
have I got?	Yes, I have./No, I haven't.
have you got?	Yes, you have./No, you haven't.
has he/she/it got?	Yes, he/she/it has./ No, he/she/it hasn't.
have we got?	Yes, we have./No, we haven't.
have they got?	Yes, they have./No, they haven't.

Present simple tense – singular

AFFIRMATIVE
I work
you work
he/she/it works

Question words
How many?

Conjunction
because

Prepositions
in a flat
near/next to/opposite the station
between the door and the window
at the back/front
on the ground floor
at weekends

Modal: *'d*
he'd like

See the Grammar Reference section at the back of the book for more information.

6 Meet the family

Focus

- Family relationships
- Further practice: people's lives, age

- Present simple tense: negative, interrogative and short answers
- Further practice: present simple tense: affirmative, questions: *Who?, What?, Where?, Which?, How old?*

Relatives

1 James is at Tom Hall's house for dinner. Listen and write the names of Tom's family. Choose from these names:

Sally Bob Barbara Kate John

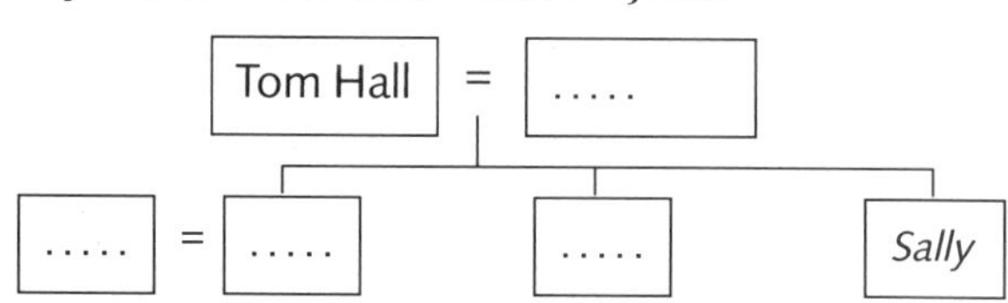

2 Now answer the questions.

Who is Barbara's husband? *Tom.*

1 Who is John's wife?
2 Who is Kate's brother?
3 Who is Tom's son?
4 Who are Barbara's daughters?

3 Listen and read. Are these sentences true or false?

1 Kate and John live in London.
2 Kate works in a school.
3 Kate works in London.
4 John works in a bank.
5 John works in Oxford.

James is talking to Kate after dinner.

BARBARA: Coffee, Kate?
KATE: No, thanks, Mum. I don't drink coffee in the evening.
JAMES: Do you live here, Kate?
TOM: No, James. They don't live here!
KATE: We live in Oxford.
JAMES: Ah. What do you do?
KATE: I'm a teacher.
JAMES: Do you have any children?
KATE: Yes. A boy and a girl.
JAMES: Are you their teacher?
KATE: No, they don't go to school. My son's four and my daughter's two.
JAMES: Oh, I see. And what does John do?
KATE: He works for the Bank of England.
JAMES: In Oxford?
KATE: No. We live in Oxford, and I work in Oxford, but he works in London.

4 Work in pairs. Student B is Kate's husband, John. Ask and answer. Use the information above to help you.

Where/live?
A: *Where do you live?*
B: *I live in Oxford.*

1 Where/work?
2 What/do?
3 What/wife/do?

5 Now ask and answer questions about Sally and her friend Lucy.

Where/live? (north London)

A: *Where do they live?*
B: *They live in north London.*

1 Where/go to school? (Finchley Comprehensive School)
2 What/do after school? (play tennis and volleyball)
3 What/do at weekends? (visit friends, go to discos)
4 Which languages/study? (French and German)
5 Which instruments/play? (the piano and the guitar)

6 Look at the picture of Bob, Tom's son. Guess his age and job. Guess where he is.

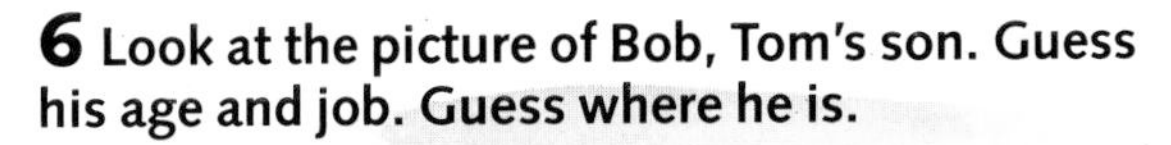

7 Work in pairs.

Student A: Read about Bob Hall and answer your partner's questions. Then ask about his girlfriend.
Student B: Turn to page 118. Ask about Bob Hall.

Bob Hall is twenty-three. He's an artist. He lives with his parents, but he's got a small studio near his parents' house. He works in the studio. At weekends he visits his girlfriend.

A: *What's her name?*
B: ...
A: *How old is she?*
B: ...
A: *Where does she live?*
B: ...

1 What/name?
2 How old?
3 Where/live?
4 Where/work?
5 What/do?

8 Now ask your partner about his/her life.

DISCOVERING LANGUAGE

9 Study the language in Exercises 3–7. Then complete the chart with the verb forms of the present simple tense.

	I/YOU/WE/THEY	HE/SHE/IT
Affirmative	.....	.....
Negative	.....	*doesn't live*
Interrogative	.....	.....

10 Pronunciation. Listen to the sound /ɜː/ in these words.

work first nurse

Listen again and repeat.

Now listen to the sound /ɔː/ in these words.

sport morning Portugal

Listen again and repeat.

Now listen to these words. Have they got an /ɜː/ sound (1) or an /ɔː/ sound (2)?

daughter Turkey thirty forty passport
water surname her wall

11 Work with a partner. Write the names of a married couple in your family. Then ask questions about your partner's relatives.

Who are they? How old is he/she?
Where do they live? What does he/she do?
Where do they work?

12 Tell the class about your partner's relatives. Then write a paragraph like the one below.

Pia is Giovanna's sister and Lorenzo is Pia's husband. Pia is twenty-two and Lorenzo is twenty-four. They live in Venice. She is a photographer and he is a journalist. He works in a newspaper office in the city centre. She works in different places.

13 Read about other students' relatives. Ask questions.

A: *Giovanna, do your sister and her husband live in a flat?*
B: *Yes, they do.*
A: *Does your sister work with her husband?*
B: *No, she doesn't.*

Birthdays

Focus

- Ordinal numbers
- Months of the year
- Dates
- Birthdays
- Further practice: family relationships

- Giving opinions of people/objects

- Question: *When?*
- Prepositions: *in* + month, *on* + date
- Adverb: *very*
- Demonstrative pronouns/ determiners: *this, that, these, those*

1 Look at James's family tree and make sentences with the words below.

Sheila is James's mother.

mother father sister brother daughter son grandmother grandfather aunt uncle niece nephew granddaughter grandson cousin children parents

2 Listen and repeat the dates.

January 1st	(January the first)
February 2nd	(February the second)
March 3rd	(March the third)
April 4th	(April the fourth)
May 5th	(May the fifth)
June 6th	(June the sixth)
July 7th	(July the seventh)
August 8th	(August the eighth)
September 9th	(September the ninth)
October 10th	(October the tenth)
November 11th	(November the eleventh)
December 12th	(December the twelfth)

3 Pronunciation. Listen and repeat the sound /θ/ in these words.

fourth fifth sixth seventh eighth

Now listen and repeat the sound /ð/ in these words.

father mother grandfather this that

Now listen to these words. Have they got a /θ/ sound (1) or a /ð/ sound (2)?

birthday grandmother thank you think they there bathroom

4 Ask and answer about the birthdays in James's family.

A: *When's his mother's birthday?*
B: *It's in March./It's on March 14th.*

5 Find two people in your class with a birthday in the same month.

A: *When's your birthday?*
B: *It's in April./It's on April 25th.*

6 Now tell the class.

Sabine's birthday's on July 3rd.
Karl's birthday's on July 7th.
So they've both got birthdays in July.

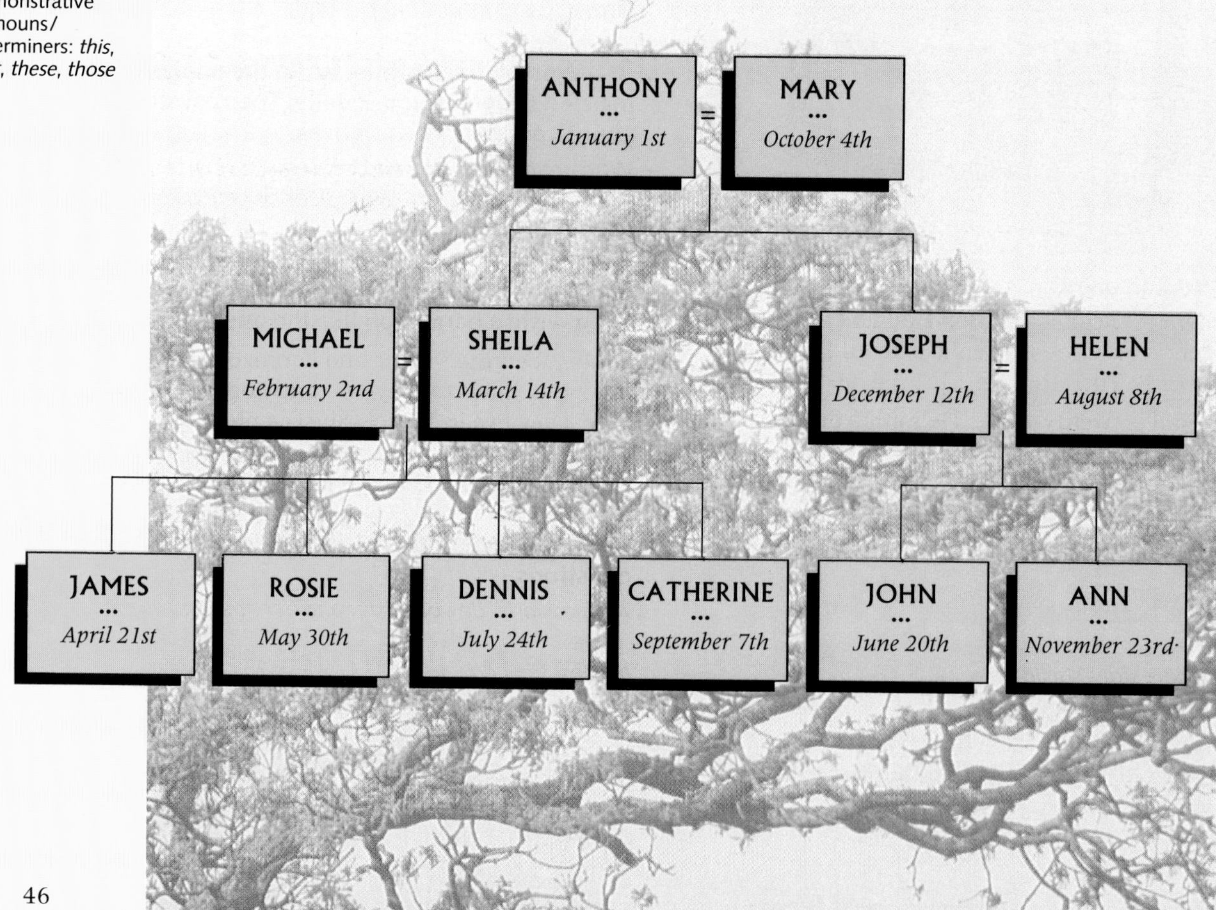

Saying what you think

1 James and Rita are looking at family photographs and talking about their relatives. Look at the photos and read what they say.

These are my cousins. They're very nice.
This is my mother. She's very kind.
This is my father. He's very strict.
This is my little sister. She's very funny.
These are my brothers. They're very handsome.
This is my aunt. She's very beautiful.
This is my father. He's a teacher. He's very interesting.

2 Tell your partner about some of your relatives.

This is my aunt. She's . . . / My aunt is . . .

3 It's Cathy's birthday. Look at four of her presents and read her opinion of them.

I think this dress is beautiful, but these shoes are ugly.

I think that poster's great because it's interesting, but those cassettes are awful.

DISCOVERING LANGUAGE

4 What are the rules for *this, that, these* and *those*?

5 Now ask and answer about the rest of Cathy's presents.

1

A: *What do you think of this book?*
B: *I think it's boring.*

2
3
4
5

Describing people

Focus

- People's appearance
- Describing people
- *What does/do ... look like?*
- Adjective position and order
- Further practice: verb *have got*

1 Look at the people above. Ask and answer about the people.

A: *What does Jerry/Jackie/Jimmy look like?*

B: *He's/She's* { *tall. / short. / bald. / fat. / thin. / black. / white.* }

C: *He's/She's got* { { *long / short* } { *black / brown / blond / red* } *hair.* / *a moustache.* / *a beard.* / *glasses.* }

2 Stress and intonation. Listen and repeat.

She's got long black hair.

He's got short blond hair.

He's got a short brown beard.

He's got a long black moustache.

She's got short red hair.

3 Listen and read. Rosie's at a party. She's talking to her friend Fiona about another friend, Tariq. Look at the picture below. Is Tariq at the party?

FIONA: Hi, Rosie!
ROSIE: Hello, Fiona.
FIONA: Come in.
ROSIE: Thanks.
FIONA: Everyone's in the garden.
ROSIE: Fiona, is Tariq here?
FIONA: Tariq? What does he look like?
ROSIE: You know. He's tall, and he's got black hair. He's got a moustache and glasses.

4 Listen to the rest of the conversation and name three other people at the party.

Listen again and look at the picture. Match the three names with three numbers.

5 Work in pairs. Look at the picture of the party.

Student A: Choose a person. Do not tell your partner. Give short answers to his/her questions.
Student B: Ask questions. Guess which person your partner is thinking of.

A: *Is it a man?*
B: *Yes, it is.*
A: *Has he got black hair?*
B: *Yes, he has.*
A: *Has he got brown eyes?*
B: *I don't know.*
A: *Has he got a moustache?*
B: *No, he hasn't.*
A: *It's Number 8!*
B: *Yes, it is.*

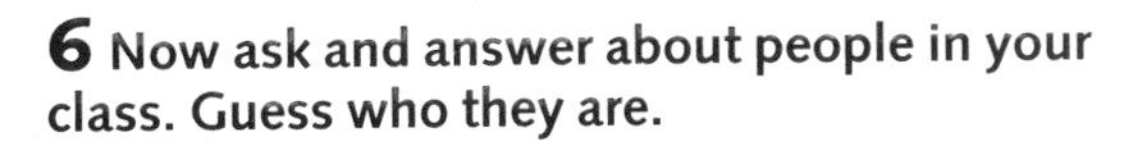

6 Now ask and answer about people in your class. Guess who they are.

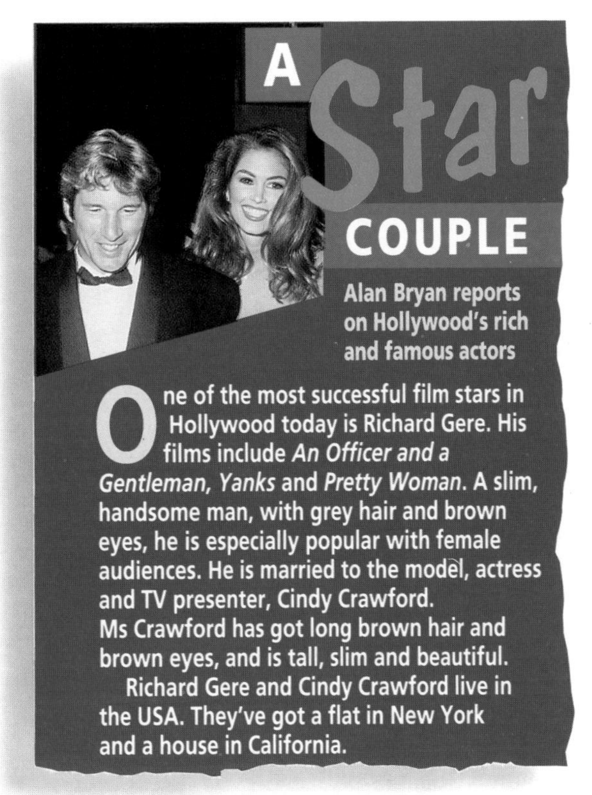

A Star COUPLE

Alan Bryan reports on Hollywood's rich and famous actors

One of the most successful film stars in Hollywood today is Richard Gere. His films include *An Officer and a Gentleman, Yanks* and *Pretty Woman*. A slim, handsome man, with grey hair and brown eyes, he is especially popular with female audiences. He is married to the model, actress and TV presenter, Cindy Crawford. Ms Crawford has got long brown hair and brown eyes, and is tall, slim and beautiful.

Richard Gere and Cindy Crawford live in the USA. They've got a flat in New York and a house in California.

7 Read about Richard Gere and Cindy Crawford. Then write questions for the answers below.

No, he isn't. He's handsome.
Is he ugly?

1 He's slim and he's got grey hair.
2 No, he hasn't. He's got brown eyes.
3 No, he hasn't. And he hasn't got a moustache.
4 Yes, he is. He's married to Cindy Crawford.
5 She's a model, actress and TV presenter.
6 No, she hasn't. She's got long brown hair.
7 In the United States.

8 Read this note. Then write a similar note describing someone in your class. Read your partner's description. Guess who it describes.

Meet me at the station at eight o'clock this evening. Come to the newsagent's. Carry a green bag and a red rose.

I'm quite tall and I've got long brown hair and brown eyes. I've also got glasses.

Development

SPEAKING

1 Tell your partner about yourself. Answer the questions.

1 Have you got a big family? How many people are there in your family?
2 Who lives in your house?
3 Do your relatives live near you?

2 Look at the pictures of this family and their shop in London. Say what you think.

1 What does the shop sell?
2 Where do these things come from?
3 Who buys clothes like these?
4 Where is this family from?
5 Picture B is Shashi Ahluwalia. Picture C is Kiran, his wife. Picture D is the Ahluwalia family. The old man is Shashi's father. Who are the other people?

LISTENING

3 Listen and choose the correct answer.

1 The textiles come from:
  a) China, India and Japan
  b) Pakistan, France and India
  c) France, Japan and India
2 The women in the family:
  a) buy the fabric
  b) sell the fabric
  c) make the fabric
3 Shashi's parents live:
  a) with Shashi
  b) with Shashi's brother
  c) alone
4 Where are they from? Match the names with the countries.
  a) Shashi and his brother — the Punjab, India
  b) Shashi's children — Nairobi, Kenya
  c) Shashi's parents — Britain

SPEAKING

4 Work with a partner. Answer the questions.

1 Do the members of your family work together like the Ahluwalias?
2 Do you know a family like them?
3 Where do they work? What do they do?

READING

5 Read the article and complete the graph.

Families in Britain

The majority of people in Britain live in small family groups. More than a quarter (26 per cent) of houses in Britain have only got one person in them. Some of these are old people but some are people in their twenties and thirties who choose to live alone. Thirty-five per cent of houses have two people in them, and another 17 per cent have three people. Fifteen per cent have four people in them, and the other homes have five or more.

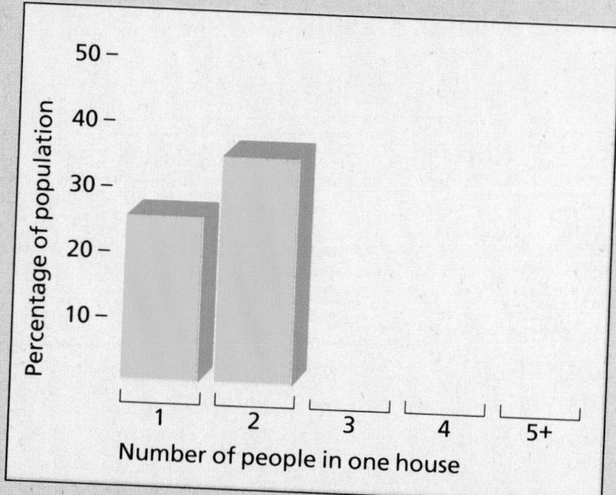

British families are small. It is unusual for couples to have more than two children. When children are about eighteen or nineteen they leave their parents' home, and they often go to a different city. Sometimes they only visit their parents two or three times a year.

COMPARING CULTURES

6 Answer the questions.

1 How big are families in your country?
2 How old are children when they leave their parents' home in your country?

WRITING: A description

7 Write about your family.

PARAGRAPH 1
Describe your family.
There are six people in my family ...

PARAGRAPH 2
Describe one member of your family (name, age, job, physical description, personality).

Summary

FUNCTIONAL LANGUAGE

Describing family relationships
Bob is Kate's brother.

Talking about jobs
What do you do?
I'm a teacher.

Talking about dates/birthdays
When's your birthday?
In September./
On September 5th.

Giving opinions
I think it's ugly.

Describing people
She's kind.
What does he look like?
He's bald and he's got a beard.

GRAMMAR

Present simple tense

AFFIRMATIVE	NEGATIVE FULL FORM	SHORT FORM
I work	I do not work	I don't work
you work (sing. and pl.)	you do not work	you don't work
he/she/it works	he/she/it does not work	he/she/it doesn't work
we work	we do not work	we don't work
they work	they do not work	they don't work

INTERROGATIVE	SHORT ANSWERS
do I work?	Yes, I do./No, I don't.
do you work?	Yes, you do./No, you don't.
does he/she/it work ?	Yes, he/she/it does./ No, he/she/it doesn't.
do we work?	Yes, we do./No, we don't.
do they work?	Yes, they do./No, they don't.

Adjectives: position and order before a noun

SIZE	COLOUR	NOUN
short	blond	hair

Ordinal numbers
first second, etc.

Question word
When?

Prepositions
in July
on July 7th

Adverb
very

Demonstrative pronouns/determiners
this that
these those

See the Grammar Reference section at the back of the book for more information.

Progress check 2

Vocabulary

1 What is this person buying? Make a list.

1 a packet of tea

2 Find the word that is different.

apples grapes milk oranges

Milk is different.

1 beef turkey salt lamb
2 rice butter cheese yoghurt
3 apples peas potatoes onions

3 Label the floors of the hotel.

A the ground floor
B the first floor

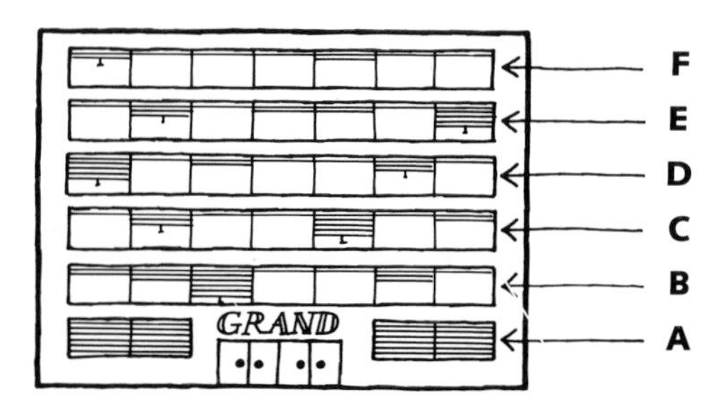

4 Match the rooms with the furniture.

bedroom – bed

sofa shower kitchen sitting room armchair toilet bedroom cooker fridge bathroom bed

5 Write about this family.

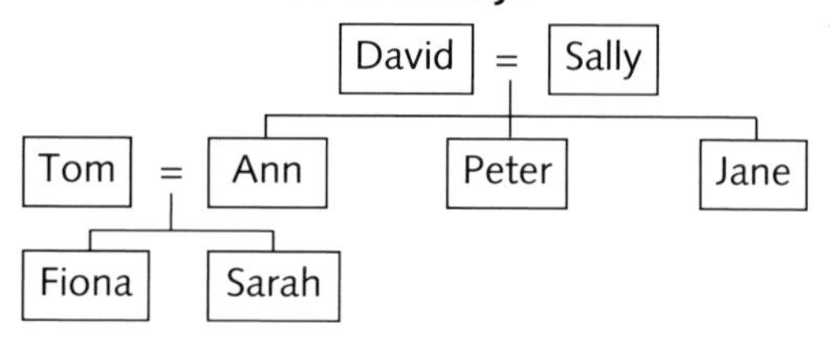

Tom/Ann

Tom is Ann's husband.

1 Ann/Tom
2 Tom and Ann/Fiona
3 Sarah/Fiona
4 Sally/Sarah
5 Peter/Fiona
6 Fiona/David

6 Write the missing months.

1 January
2 .....
3 March
4 April
5 .....
6 June
7 .....
8 August
9 September
10 October
11 .....
12 December

Grammar and functions

7 Look at the plan of the ground floor of James's hotel. Then complete the sentences with *in, next to, opposite* and *between.*

1 The dining room is ..... the reception desk.
2 The telephones are ..... the coffee bar.
3 The coffee bar is ..... the dining room.
4 The manager's office is ..... the shop and the reception desk.
5 The shop is ..... the manager's office.

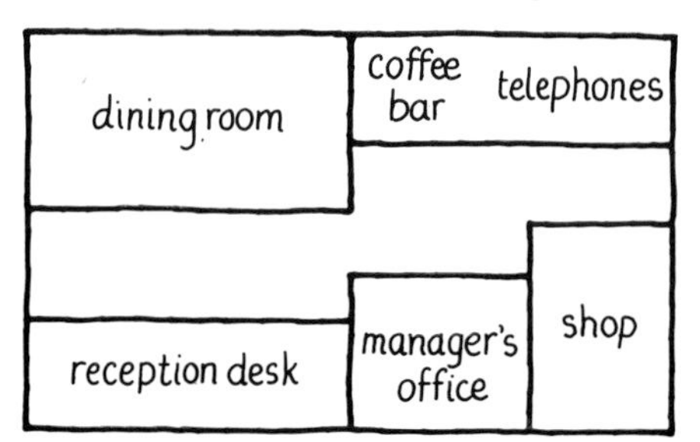

8 **Complete the conversation with *a, some* or *any*.**

A: Hello. Have you got (1) ..... apples?
B: Yes. How many would you like?
A: Two pounds, please. And I'd like (2) ..... bananas – about six.
B: Anything else?
A: Yes. (3) ..... bottle of milk, please, and (4) ..... bread.
B: Sorry. There isn't (5) ..... bread.
A: Oh. Can I have (6) ..... packet of biscuits?
B: Yes. Here you are.
A: Thank you.

9 **Complete the questions with these words:**

What Who How much When Where

1 '..... is the party?' 'On December 1st.'
2 '..... is that?' 'That's John.'
3 '..... is that?' 'That's mayonnaise.'
4 '..... would you like to eat?' 'Spaghetti, please.'
5 '..... would you like to eat?' 'At McDonald's.'
6 '..... has got my pen?' 'I have.'
7 '..... is that?' 'One pound twenty.'

10 **Read the answers and write questions. Use the word(s) in brackets.**

(you) I'm a teacher.
What do you do?

1 (Bob) In his parents' house.
2 (Alan and Rosie) At Brighton General Hospital.
3 (Pia) Italian, French and English.
4 (you) We go to discos.
5 (Alan) The saxophone.

11 **Maria is talking to a man at a party. She doesn't want to speak to him so she's giving very short answers to his questions. Write what she says.**

Do you live in Brighton?
Yes, I do.

1 'Are you a friend of Rosie's?' 'Yes, ...'
2 'Do you work at the hospital?' 'No, ...'
3 'Do you know Rosie's brother, James?' 'Yes, ...'
4 'Are you Spanish?' 'No, ...'
5 'Have you got a flat in Brighton?' 'No, ...'
6 'Do you like Britain?' 'Yes, ...'

12 **Read the sentences about Rosie. They are not true. Correct them.**

She lives in London. (Brighton)
No, she doesn't. She lives in Brighton.

1 She works in a bank. (hospital)
2 She's got a daughter. (brother)
3 Maria is her sister. (friend)
4 She lives in a hostel. (flat)
5 There are three bedrooms in her flat. (two)

Common errors

13 **Are these sentences correct (✓) or incorrect (✗)? Rewrite the incorrect ones.**

The furnitures are beautiful. ✗
The furniture is beautiful.

1 Are there any cheese in the fridge?
2 There isn't some sugar.
3 I haven't got any money.
4 There isn't a brown loaf.

14 **Choose the correct preposition.**

Maria lives **on/in** Brighton.
Maria lives in Brighton.

Maria lives (1) **in/at** a hostel (2) **on/in** the ground floor. She likes the hostel because it's (3) **in/near** the sea. She studies (4) **on/at** a language school. She visits friends (5) **at/in** weekends.

15 **Correct the mistakes.**

She studys Spanish.
She studies Spanish.

1 I am live in a flat in London.
2 She not live here.
3 Do he work in a shop?
4 No. He work in a restaurant.

16 **Choose the correct sentence, (a) or (b).**

a) His moustaches are black.
b) His moustache is black. ✓

1 a) She has got hair short and blond.
b) She has got short blond hair.
2 a) He's bald. b) He bald.
3 a) He got a beard. b) He's got a beard.
4 a) I've got long brown hair.
b) I've got brown long hair.

At the end of the Progress Check, look back at your mistakes and study the Grammar Reference section if you need more help.

7 Shopping

Shops

Focus

- Shops
- Toiletries
- Clothes
- Containers

- *'s* for shops
- Irregular plural: *teeth*
- Further practice: verb *have got*, present simple tense, determiner: *any*

Packing list
dress
T-shirts
soap
sandwiches
sweets
toothbrush
sweater
writing paper
coat
tickets
jeans
shirt
shoes
towel
camera
Walkman
jacket
make-up
magazines
chocolate
tissues
toothpaste
shampoo
diary
money
envelopes
socks
tights
pyjamas
books
umbrella
films
batteries

1 Rosie and Maria are going to visit Ireland. Compare Rosie's packing list with the picture and say what she hasn't got. Use a dictionary to help you.

She hasn't got a dress.
She hasn't got any sandwiches.
She hasn't got any writing paper.

2 Find words in Rosie's list to add to the diagrams. Add any other words you know.

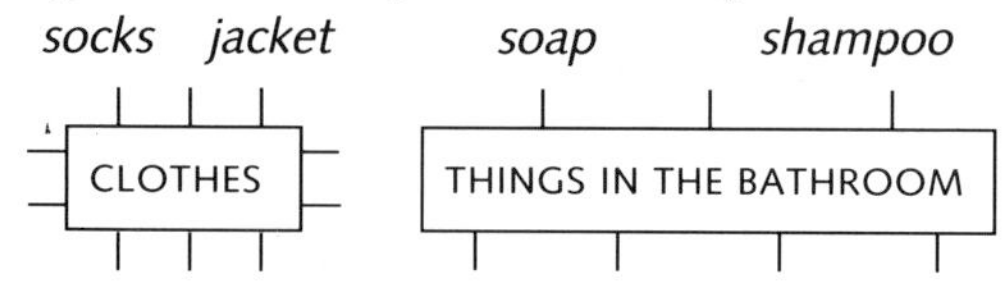

3 Match the sentences with words from Rosie's list.

I read these. There are photographs in them. – *magazines*

1 I write in this every day.
2 I wash my hair with this.
3 I wear this in the house when it's cold.
4 I put these in my camera.
5 I eat this, but it isn't good for my teeth!
6 I wear these on my feet every day.

4 Work with a partner. Answer the questions.

1 What do these shops sell? Make lists.
They sell soap, shampoo and ... at the chemist's.
2 Which shops sell the things that Rosie wants? Tell the class.
Rosie wants ... They sell ... at the chemist's.

5 Look again at Rosie's list. Match the words below with some of the things on her list.

a bar of soap

1 bar 2 packet 3 bottle 4 tube 5 box

COMPARING CULTURES

6 Say where you buy these things in your country.

In France we buy ... at a ...

1 batteries 4 newspapers
2 cakes 5 toothpaste
3 sweaters 6 cheese

7 Listen to three conversations. Match them with the pictures.

What do you notice about the conversations? Is it the same in your country?

ENGLISH AROUND YOU

Buying things

Focus

- Shopping
- Containers
- Quantities

- Specifying particular things
- Asking for clarification
- Further practice: asking for something, buying things, asking prices

- Pronouns: *one, ones*
- Questions: *Which one(s)?, How many?* (countable), *How much?* (uncountable)
- Further practice: *this, that, these, those, I'd like . . . ,* questions: *Which?, Can I have . . . ?*

1 **Listen and read. Sally is in a shop. Complete the conversation.**

ASSISTANT: Morning. Can I help you?
SALLY: Yes, I'd like (1) . . . . . , please. And do you sell stamps?
ASSISTANT: Yes. How many would you like?
SALLY: (2) . . . . . , please.
ASSISTANT: Anything else?
SALLY: Yes. Can I have (3) . . . . . , please?
ASSISTANT: Certainly. Which one?
SALLY: That one.
ASSISTANT: This one?
SALLY: No, the red one. Over there. Oh, and how much are those files?
ASSISTANT: Which ones?
SALLY: The big blue ones, between the writing paper and the notebooks.
ASSISTANT: (4) . . . . . each.
SALLY: Right. Can I have two, please?
ASSISTANT: Of course. Anything else?
SALLY: No, that's it, thanks. How much is that altogether?
ASSISTANT: That's (5) . . . . . , please.
SALLY: Here you are.
ASSISTANT: Thanks. (6) . . . . . change.
SALLY: Thank you. Bye.
ASSISTANT: Bye.

2 **Now answer the questions.**

1 What kind of a shop is Sally in?
2 What does she buy?
3 How much is it altogether?
4 How much does Sally give the shop assistant?
5 How much is the change?

3 **You are in the shop above. Ask and answer about the things on the counter.**

A: *I'd like a(n) . . . , please.*
B: *Which one?*
A: *This/that one, please.*
A: *I'd like some . . . , please.*
B: *Which ones?*
A: *These/those, please.*

4 **Now ask and answer about the things on the shelves.**

A: *Can I have a(n)? . . . , please.*
B: *Which one would you like?*
A: *The big green one, please.*
A: *Can I have some . . . , please?*
B: *Which ones would you like?*
A: *The small brown ones, please.*

5 **Work in pairs.**

Student A: You are a customer in the shop above. Buy three things.
Greet the shop assistant.
Ask if he/she sells what you want.
Choose what you want.
Ask the price and buy the things.
Student B: You are a shop assistant in the shop above. Turn to page 119.

DISCOVERING LANGUAGE

6 Read the conversations and answer the questions.

> Can I have some cheese, please?
>
> Yes. How much would you like?
>
> I'd like some bottles of orange juice, please.
>
> Certainly. How many do you want?

1 Two nouns in the conversations are *cheese* and *bottles*. Which noun is countable? Which one is uncountable?
2 Which word, *much* or *many*, do we use in questions about countable nouns? Which word do we use in questions about uncountable nouns?

7 Work with a partner. Plan what to buy for a class party. There are some ideas in the pictures. Decide about quantities. Then write a list.

A: *How much orange juice/How many bottles of orange juice do we want?*
B: *About five bottles.*

five bottles of orange juice
six litres of milk

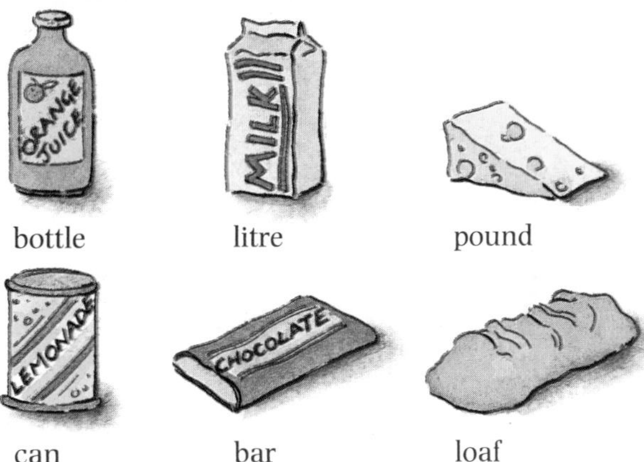

bottle litre pound
can bar loaf

Join two other students and compare your lists. Ask what they think about your list.

8 Stress and intonation. Listen and repeat.

A: Three packets of biscuits, please.
B: Sorry? How many?
A: Half a pound of cheese, please.
B: Sorry? How much?

Check these requests in the same way.

1 Half a pound of butter, please.
2 Five pens, please.
3 That's three pounds eighty.
4 Six envelopes, please.
5 Can I have two blue T-shirts, please?

Now listen and check your answers.

ENGLISH AROUND YOU

Development

SPEAKING

1 Look at Pictures A and B and answer the questions.

1 Robert Smith is a greengrocer. What does a British greengrocer sell?
2 Where do you think Robert buys the things for his shop?

LISTENING

2 Listen to Robert and check your answers to Exercise 1.

SPEAKING

3 Work in pairs. Look at Pictures A and B again. Practise conversations between Robert and his customers.

LISTENING

4 Listen to two conversations in Robert's shop. Match them with the pictures. Then complete the chart.

	ITEM	PRICE	QUANTITY WANTED
Customer 1	grapes	£1.00 a pound	a bunch
	.....	..... each	.....
Customer 2	.....	..... a pound	.....
	.....	..... a pound	.....
	.....	..... each	.....
	.....	______	.....

READING

5 Look at the advertisements above for shops in the Brighton area.

1 Name a shop where you can buy:
   a) a piano
   b) books
   c) flowers
   d) a computer
   e) tennis balls
   f) a sleeping bag
2 Name the shop(s) in each of these places:
   a) Forest Row
   b) Horsham
   c) Burgess Hill
   d) Brighton
   e) Goring by Sea
3 You want to buy a tent and you need some information.
   a) What number do you phone if you are in Forest Row?
   b) What number do you phone if you are in another town?
   c) What questions would you like to ask the shop assistant?

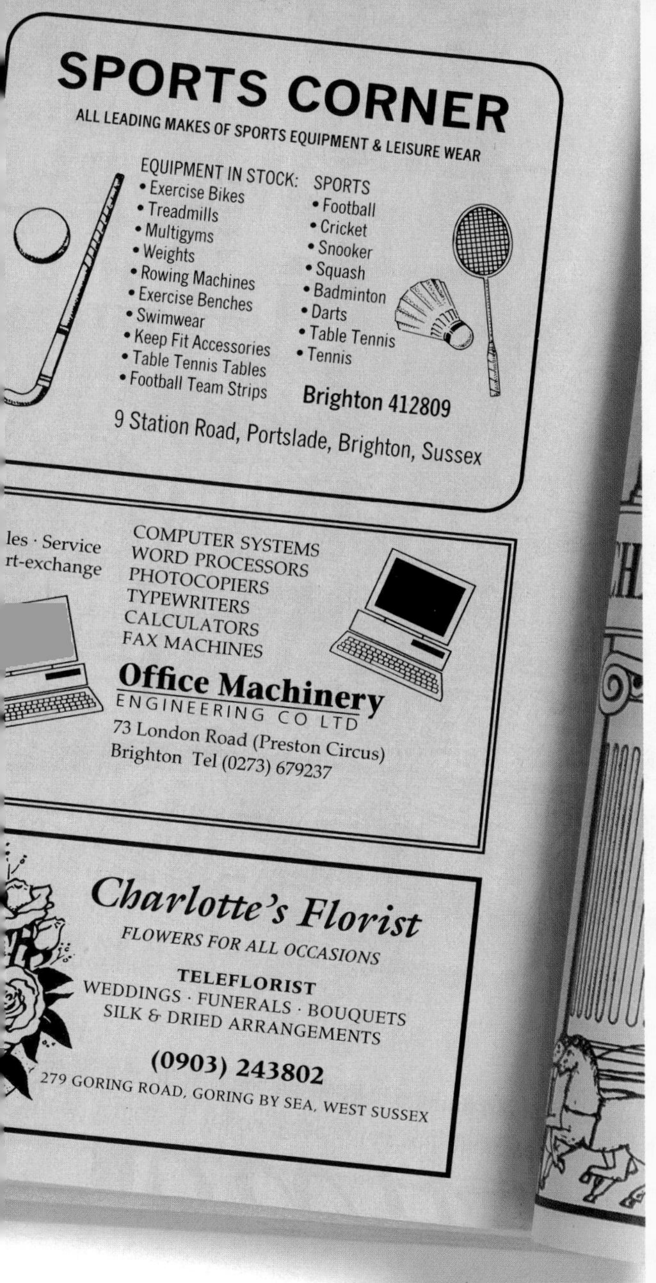

WRITING

6 **You and your partner are visiting a friend in the mountains for a week. Write a packing list. Include all the things you want to take.**

SPEAKING

7 **Read your partner's list. Discuss the differences and add things to your list if necessary. Decide which things to buy. Which shops sell these things?**

Summary

FUNCTIONAL LANGUAGE

Talking about what shops sell
They sell magazines at the newsagent's.

Responding to thanks
Don't mention it./That's OK.

Asking for things in shops
I'd like some envelopes, please.
Can I have a file, please?
Do you sell stamps?

Asking for clarification
Which one/ones?
Sorry? *How* many?/*How* much?
Sorry? *Which* page?

GRAMMAR

***'s* for shops**
a/the chemist's
a/the newsagent's

one/ ones

Which one?	Which ones?
This/that one.	These/those.
The red one.	The red ones.

Question words
How many + countable noun
How much + uncountable noun

Irregular plural form
tooth teeth

See the Grammar Reference section at the back of the book for more information.

8 Daily life

Routines

Focus

- Telling the time
- Talking about routines

- Question: *What time?*
- Prepositions: *at* + time, *at* + place, *by* + transport
- Adverbs of frequency
- Zero article: *at home, to work, by train*
- Further practice: present simple tense

1 Ask and answer about the clocks below.

A: *What time is it?*
B: *It's two o'clock.*

It's two o'clock. It's half past nine. It's quarter past one.

It's quarter to six. It's twenty past eleven.

2 James and Julia are at the office. They're watching an advertisement for Beta Clocks. Look at the pictures of the advertisement above and listen. Match the pictures with the expressions below. Which picture is missing?

Picture 1 – get up

have dinner start work go to bed
get up have breakfast finish work
go to school come home watch TV

3 Ask and answer about the Kay family.

A: *What time does Bill get up?*
B: *He gets up at seven o'clock.*

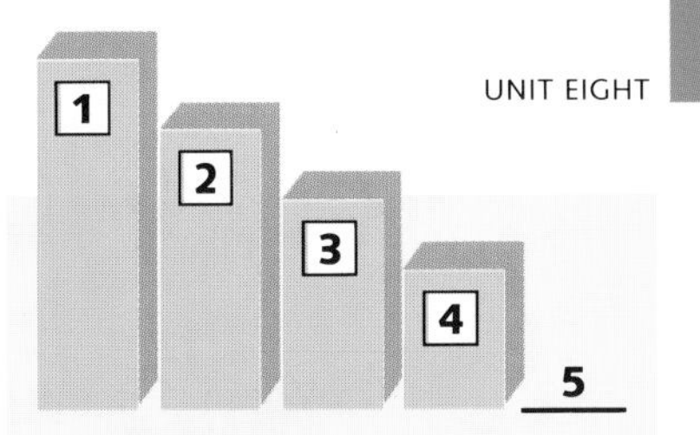

DISCOVERING LANGUAGE

5 Match the adverbs below with the blocks in the chart.

1 – always

always never often
sometimes usually

6 Pronunciation. Listen and repeat the expressions. Notice: at = /ət/; to = /tə/.

at home at six o'clock
at school at half past two
at work to work to school
to college by car by train
by bus by bicycle

DISCOVERING LANGUAGE

7 Look at the expressions in Exercise 6. What rule can you make about the use of the definite article (*the*) in these expressions?

4 Match the occupations with the texts.

student waiter businesswoman postman

1 " I start work at nine. I finish at about seven. I often work late, and I sometimes work at home too. I usually have lunch in a restaurant because my company pays. I always wear smart clothes, like a suit, to work. I go to work by train. I never go by car – there's too much traffic. "

2 " My job is an evening job. I start at six o'clock in the evening and finish at about two o'clock in the morning. I have a break at about ten and I always eat in the kitchen. I wear a uniform, of course. "

3 " I go in when there are classes. They sometimes start at nine, sometimes at ten. I usually have lunch in the cafeteria, but some days I don't have lunch. In the evenings I often work in the library. I go everywhere by bicycle. I usually wear casual clothes like jeans. "

4 " I start early – at five o'clock in the morning – and I usually finish at about one o'clock in the afternoon, so I always have lunch at home. I wear a uniform at work. "

8 Ask your partner about his/her habits. Here are some questions and expressions to help you:

A: *What time do you get up?*
B: *At half past seven.*
A: *Where do you work/study?*
B: *In a shop/At university.*
A: *What do you wear?*
B: *Smart clothes/Casual clothes/ A uniform.*
A: *When/where do you eat?*
B: *At college/At home/In a café.*
A: *How do you travel?*
B: *By train/By bicycle/On foot.*

9 Write five sentences comparing your day with your partner's.

I always get up at half past six, but Steffi usually gets up at eight.

Clocks and calendars

Focus

- Times of the day
- Timetables
- Days of the week

- Further practice: talking about routines

- Prepositions: *in* + time, *in* + year, *on* + day
- Further practice: present simple tense, question: *What time?*, *on* + date, *in* + month

1 What is the difference between 8 a.m. and 8 p.m.? Look at the chart and check your answer.

a.m.	morning	00.00–11.59
p.m.	afternoon evening	12.00–17.59 18.00–23.59
NOTE:	00.00 = midnight 12.00 = midday (noon)	

2 Match the times that are the same.

03.00 – 3 a.m. – three o'clock in the morning

1 03.00	8 a.m.	one o'clock in the morning
2 15.00	1 a.m.	eight o'clock in the evening
3 20.00	3 a.m. →	three o'clock in the morning
4 01.00	1 p.m.	eight o'clock in the morning
5 13.00	3 p.m.	one o'clock in the afternoon
6 08.00	8 p.m.	three o'clock in the afternoon

3 Look at the information below and complete the sentences. Write the time with *a.m.* or *p.m.*

1 The café opens ...
2 The film starts ...
3 The café closes ...
4 The film finishes ...
5 The plane arrives ...
6 The plane leaves ...

Odeon Cinema, King Street
ROBIN HOOD
PRINCE OF THIEVES
Special showing every day this week
15.00
(running time 140 minutes)
THE CINEMA
Café
Open 12.00–23.30 7 days a week
Come in for a snack before or after going next door to the cinema!
We serve hot and cold drinks, fresh sandwiches and salads, and home-made pastries and cakes.
Date 3rd July
Destination Milan
Flight number BA564
Departure 11.30
Arrival 14.35
your tickets

COMPARING CULTURES

4 List places in your country where they use the 24-hour clock.

5 Look at the calendar.

1 Listen and repeat the days of the week.
2 Ask and answer about the days.

A: *What day is May 15th?*
B: *It's a Wednesday.*

MAY					
Monday		6	13	20	27
Tuesday		7	14	21	28
Wednesday	1	8	15	22	29
Thursday	2	9	16	23	30
Friday	3	10	17	24	31
Saturday	4	11	18	25	
Sunday	5	12	19	26	

6 Listen to Sally Hall and answer the questions.

1 Which day does she: usually play tennis; often go to a club; visit her grandmother?
2 Does she like Mondays? Why (not)?
3 Which days are 'the weekend' in Britain?

DISCOVERING LANGUAGE

7 Read the sentences. What rules can you make about the use of *in, on* and *at* for talking about time?

1 They get up at eight o'clock in the morning.
2 She always works late on Tuesdays.
3 My birthday's in May.
4 School starts on September 5th.
5 In 1996 February has twenty-nine days.

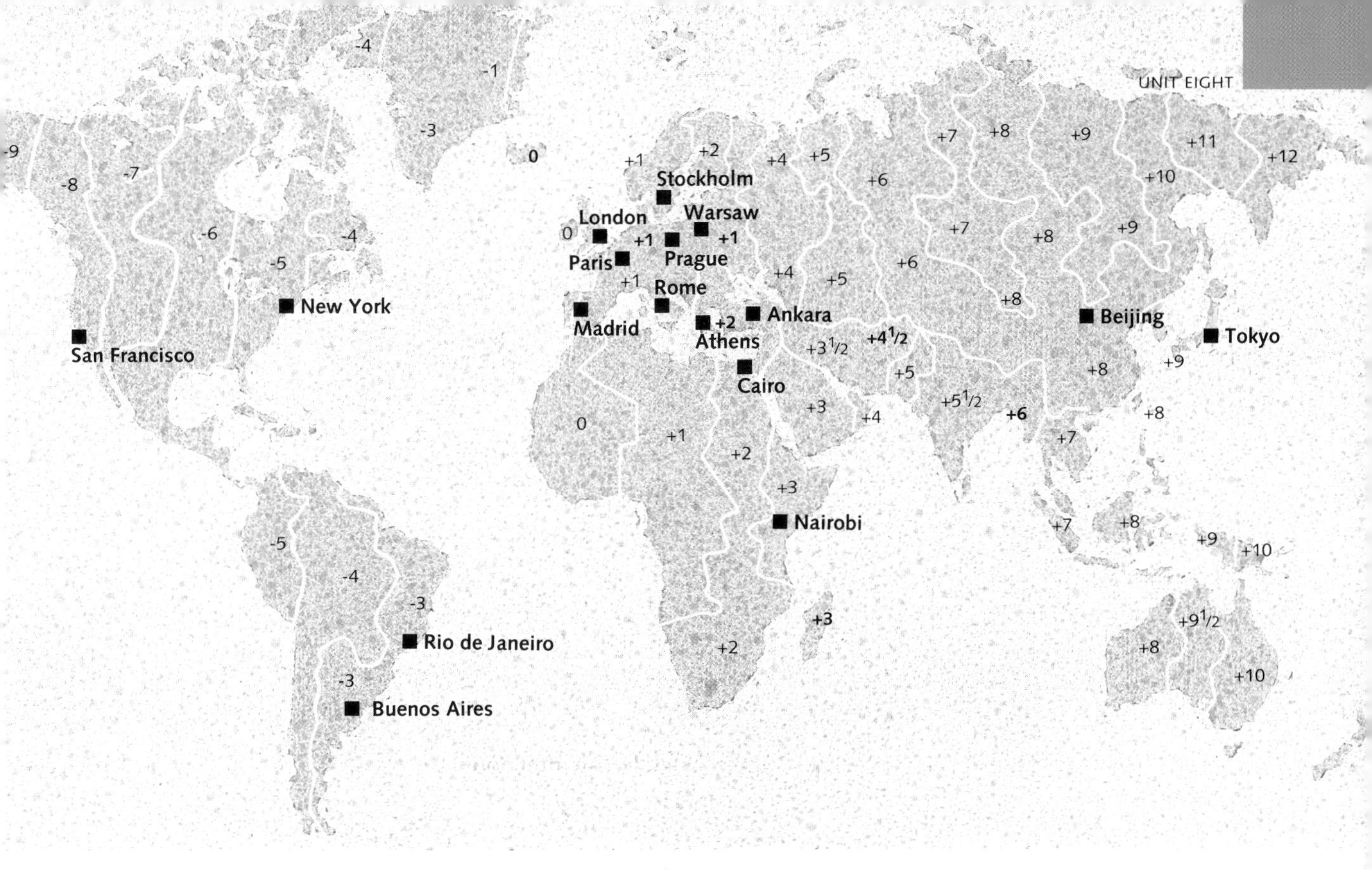

8 Complete the sentences with *in*, *at* or *on*.

1 The party is ..... Friday.
2 The shop opens ..... 9.30 ..... the morning.
3 The meeting is ..... August 25th.
4 It's always cold ..... January.
5 Her twenty-first birthday is ..... 1999.

9 Look at the map of international time zones above and complete the chart with the correct times. Then make sentences.

When it's midday in London, it's 1 p.m. in Paris.

PLACE	TIME	PLACE	TIME
1 London	midday	Paris	1 p.m.
2 Rome	5 a.m.	Tokyo	.....
3 Athens	2 p.m.	Rio de Janeiro	.....
4 Paris	midnight	Nairobi	.....
5 Prague	.....	Beijing	6 a.m.
6 Warsaw	.....	Buenos Aires	11 p.m.
7 Ankara	7 p.m.	New York	.....

Now answer the questions.

1 Your plane leaves London at 8.20 a.m. for Cairo. The flight is five hours. What time do you arrive in Cairo (Egyptian time)?
2 You are in Stockholm. You want to phone your sister in San Francisco at 7 a.m. her time. What time do you call (Swedish time)?

COMPARING CULTURES

10 Read the text and the sentences. Are the sentences true or false? Correct the false ones.

Changing the clocks in Britain

In Britain they change the clocks twice a year. When spring begins, they put the clocks forward by one hour. This gives more hours of daylight in the evenings. In the middle of summer it gets dark at about 10 p.m.

When summer ends, they put the clocks back by one hour. This means that children go to school in daylight. In the middle of winter the sun rises late, at about 8 a.m., and sets at about 4 p.m. There are not many hours of daylight in winter.

1 When spring begins, British people change their clocks from 1 a.m. to midnight.
2 In the middle of winter there are about ten hours of daylight.
3 In winter children go to school in daylight.

11 Find expressions in the text that are similar in meaning to:

1 two times
2 the sun comes up
3 the sun goes down

12 Do you change the clocks in your country? When? Why?

SPEAKING

1 Look at the pictures. What is the building? Which country do you think it is in? Who are the people?

LISTENING

2 Listen to Part 1. Check your answers to Exercise 1 and then complete the timetable.

TIMETABLE	
.....	Breakfast
.....	Lesson 1
.....	Coffee break
11.00–12.30	.....
12.30–2.00	.....
.....	Lesson 3

3 Now listen to Parts 1 and 2. Which verbs does Marc use with these words?

..... breakfast
have breakfast

1 ..... coffee
2 ..... in the learning centre
3 ..... football
4 ..... aerobics
5 ..... films
6 ..... to the cinema

READING

4 Read this brochure from another language school and answer the questions.

1 How many students are there?
2 Is the Institute open at weekends?
3 Where do the students live?

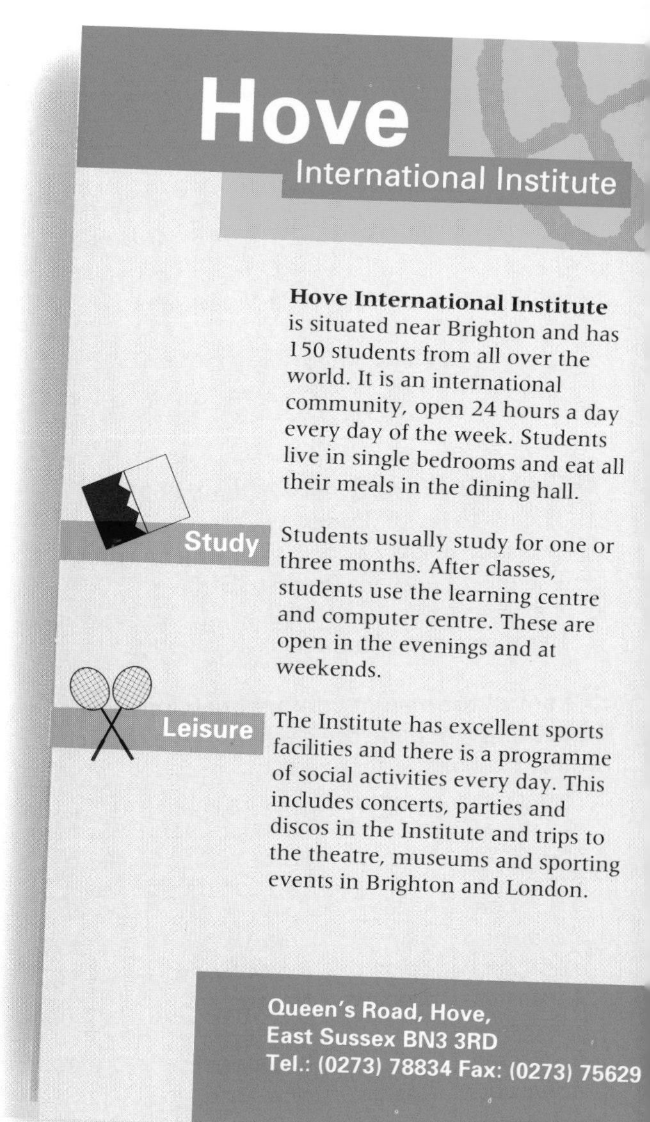

Hove
International Institute

Hove International Institute is situated near Brighton and has 150 students from all over the world. It is an international community, open 24 hours a day every day of the week. Students live in single bedrooms and eat all their meals in the dining hall.

Study Students usually study for one or three months. After classes, students use the learning centre and computer centre. These are open in the evenings and at weekends.

Leisure The Institute has excellent sports facilities and there is a programme of social activities every day. This includes concerts, parties and discos in the Institute and trips to the theatre, museums and sporting events in Brighton and London.

Queen's Road, Hove,
East Sussex BN3 3RD
Tel.: (0273) 78834 Fax: (0273) 75629

LISTENING

5 Now listen to a telephone conversation with the secretary of the Institute. Answer the questions.

1 Where is the student from?
2 When does he want to do a course?
3 Is it possible?

SPEAKING

6 Work in pairs.

Student A: You want to be a student at the Institute for one month in July or August. You want to stay with a British family. Telephone the secretary and ask about: the cost of courses, the starting dates of courses and where you can stay.
Student B: You are the Institute's secretary. Turn to page 119. Answer your partner's questions.

B: *Hello, Hove International Institute. Can I help you?*
A: *Hello. I'd like to do a course at the Institute. Can you give me some information?*

WRITING: A formal letter

7 Look at the letter format and the parts of the letter below. Match the parts of the letter with the correct number on the format.

1 – C

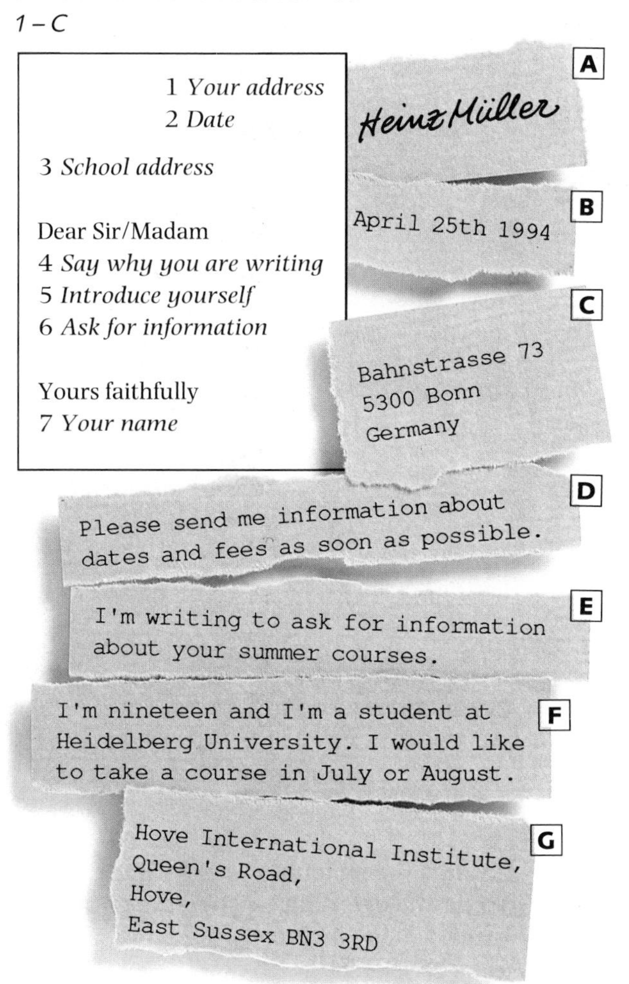
1 *Your address*
2 *Date*
3 *School address*
Dear Sir/Madam
4 *Say why you are writing*
5 *Introduce yourself*
6 *Ask for information*
Yours faithfully
7 *Your name*

A
Heinz Müller

B
April 25th 1994

C
Bahnstrasse 73
5300 Bonn
Germany

D
Please send me information about dates and fees as soon as possible.

E
I'm writing to ask for information about your summer courses.

F
I'm nineteen and I'm a student at Heidelberg University. I would like to take a course in July or August.

G
Hove International Institute,
Queen's Road,
Hove,
East Sussex BN3 3RD

Now write a similar letter to the Institute with information about yourself.

Summary

FUNCTIONAL LANGUAGE

Telling the time
What time is it?
It's one o'clock/half past two/quarter to three/quarter past four.

Talking about routines
What time/When do you get up?
At seven o'clock.
We have breakfast at eight.
She has lunch at half past twelve.

Talking about frequency
I sometimes work at home.

GRAMMAR

Adverbs of frequency
always
usually
often
sometimes
never

Prepositions
at five o'clock/home/school/work
in the morning/the afternoon/the evening/July/1996
on Tuesdays/September 5th
by car/train/bus/plane/bicycle
on foot

Zero article
at home
to work
by train

Question words
What time?

Times of the day
six a.m./p.m.
six o'clock in the morning/in the evening
06.00/18.00

See the Grammar Reference section at the back of the book for more information.

9 Spare time

Hobbies

Focus

- Hobbies/spare-time activities
- Television programmes

- Talking about likes and dislikes
- Talking about time duration
- Further practice: giving opinions

- Verb *to like* + noun/*-ing*
- Questions: *Why?, Why not?, What kind of . . . ?*
- Preposition: *for* + time

- Further practice: *because*

south coast
ARTS CENTRE BRIGHTON

Evening Classes

Why sit in front of the television? It's ***BORING!***
Do something new

Drama
Photography
Painting
Pottery
Story writing
Making videos
Dancing

Interesting!
Creative!
Fun!
Exciting!

and many more activities . . .
Courses begin October 2nd
For details, contact
Jane Wilson on **68459**.

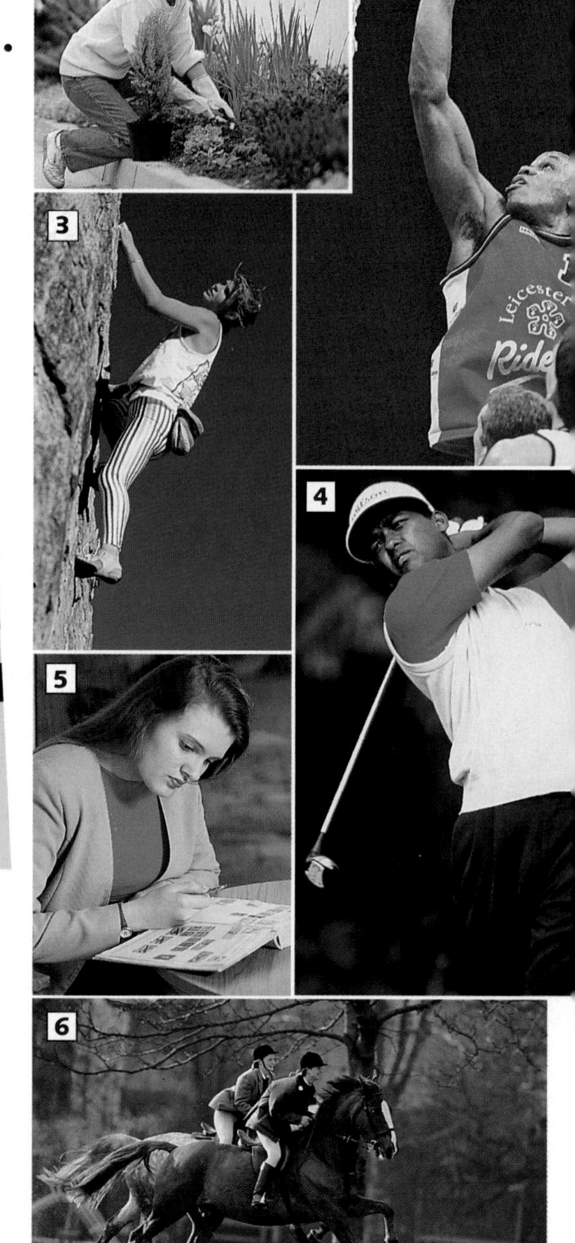

1 Read the poster and listen to the conversation.

MARIA: Hey, look at all these evening classes, Rosie.
ROSIE: Oh – story writing. I like writing. What about you?
MARIA: No, I don't like writing in English. It's difficult for me. But dancing, yes, I like that. And photography too.
ROSIE: Mm. I sometimes make videos with a friend's camera. It's really good fun. Erm . . . What else is there? Painting – no, I don't like painting. Do you?
MARIA: Not really. Actually, you know, British television isn't boring. It's good for my English.

Which activities do Maria and Rosie like doing? Which don't they like?

Maria likes photography./Maria likes taking photographs.

2 Match the pictures above with the hobbies below. Which hobbies are not included in the pictures?

Picture 1 – gardening

golf hang-gliding basketball riding gardening playing the guitar climbing collecting stamps fishing badminton

3 Use the words below to describe your feelings about each hobby in Exercise 2. Use a dictionary to help you.

I think fishing is boring.

interesting creative exciting good fun dangerous boring good exercise relaxing expensive difficult

4 Stress and intonation. Listen and repeat.

Do you like fishing? No, I don't.

Do you like riding? Yes, I do.

Why do you like riding?

Because it's good fun.

5 Ask and answer about the hobbies and make notes.

A: *Do you like fishing?*
B: *Yes, I do./No, I don't.*
A: *Why?/Why not?*
B: *Because it's relaxing/boring.*

6 Now tell the class about your partner.

Pablo likes climbing because it's exciting. He doesn't like collecting stamps because it's boring.

DISCOVERING LANGUAGE

7 Look at these pairs of words. Can you make any spelling rules for *-ing* forms?

play playing
climb climbing
swim swimming
hit hitting
ride riding
write writing

COMPARING CULTURES

8 A lot of people in Britain like watching television in their spare time. Look at the graph and make sentences to describe the information it gives.

British people between four and fifteen watch television for about eighteen hours a week.

Watching the box in Britain

KEY: [TV] = 4 hours

HOURS A WEEK: 4 8 12 16 20 24 28 32 36 40

AGE: 4-15 16-34 35-65 over 65

Do you think the graph is correct for people of your age in your country?

9 Look at the names of different kinds of television programme. Name programmes of each kind in your country.

1 sport
2 drama
3 news
4 films
5 cartoons
6 game shows
7 comedies
8 chat shows
9 nature programmes
10 soaps ('soap operas')

10 Work in groups. Use the questionnaire to ask and answer about people's viewing habits.

QUESTIONNAIRE

Are you a TV slob?

Try our quick questionnaire and find out.

1 Do you like watching TV?
2 How many hours a week do you watch TV?
3 Do you always stay at home to watch it?
4 What kind of programmes do you like?
5 What's your favourite programme?
6 What kind of programmes don't you like?

11 Tell the class about people in your group.

Elsa watches television for about twenty-five hours a week. She likes watching sport and films. She doesn't like game shows.

12 Now write about yourself in the same way.

Focus

- Talking about present activities
- Present progressive tense

Doing things

1 📼 **Listen and read. Sally is looking after her sister Kate's children and two of their friends. Kate is telephoning Sally.**

SALLY: Hello.
KATE: Hello, Sally. Is everything OK? Are you having any problems?
SALLY: No, Kate, I'm not. Everything's fine.
KATE: Good. What are you doing?
SALLY: I'm doing my homework.
KATE: And the children? What are they doing?
SALLY: Oh – they're playing a game. They aren't making a noise.
KATE: Right. And are you watching the baby?
SALLY: Yes, we are. She's fine. She's drinking her milk now.
KATE: Good. Well, see you at eight o'clock then.
SALLY: OK. Bye, Kate.

What does Sally say about these people? Complete the sentences.

'I'm ...'
'The children are ...'
'The baby is ...'

2 Look at Picture 1 and correct Sally's false statements. Use the words below to help you.

She isn't doing her homework. She's listening to music.

listen fight cry eat

DISCOVERING LANGUAGE

3 Look at the conversation again and complete the sentences with examples of the present progressive tense.

1 She ..... to music. (listen)
2 They ..... not ...... (fight)
3 What ..... you .....? (do)

How do we form the present progressive tense?

4 Look at Picture 2. Describe what is happening in Kate's house now.

Sally / do / homework
Sally is doing her homework.

1 boys / wash / walls
2 girl / watch / television
3 baby / sit / chair
4 baby / play
5 boys / not / fight
6 girl / not / cry

5 **Work in pairs. Find six differences between the picture below and the picture on page 120. Ask and answer. Use the verbs below.**

Student A: Look at the picture below.
Student B: Look at the picture on page 120.

stand talk eat drink carry wear

A: *Is there a man in your picture?*
B: *Yes, there is./No, there isn't.*
A: *Is he standing?*
B: *Yes, he is./No, he isn't.*
A: *What's he carrying?*
B: *A bag.*
A: *What colour is it?*
B: *It's ...*

6 **Look again at the picture in Exercise 5. Use your imagination and discuss the questions.**

1 How old are these people?
2 Where are they from?
3 Are they friends?
4 What is she saying?
5 Are they both catching a train?
6 Where are they going?
7 Why are they going?

7 **Write a description of the picture.**

Two friends are at a station. They are waiting ...

8 **Make teams. One student acts out an activity. The other team guesses what he/she is doing. The actor only answers *Yes* or *No.***

A: *Are you taking photographs?/You're taking photographs!*
B: *Yes, I am./No, I'm not.*

ENGLISH AROUND YOU

That's all for today. See you on Monday. Have a nice weekend!

Development

SPEAKING

1 Work with a partner. Look at the pictures and the plan of a sports centre. Say what the people are doing in each picture. Then match the activities with the places in the sports centre. Use the expressions below.

Picture 1 – They're running on the running track.

in the gym in the swimming pool in the café
on a squash court on the running track
on a tennis court in the shop

LISTENING

2 The manager of the sports centre is talking about the activities there. Listen and complete the chart.

ACTIVITY	PLACE	TIMES
Tennis	Tennis courts	9.00 a.m.– 9.00 p.m.
Athletics	Running track	.....
.....	Swimming pool	.....
Aerobics (Women)	Gym	.....
(Men)		.....
.....	Gym	1.00 p.m.– 5.00 p.m.
Fitness training	Gym	.....
Squash	.....	.....

Now listen again. Check your chart and then write down the opening hours of:

1 the sports centre 2 the shop 3 the café

1 run

2 (have) a cup of tea

3 (play) tennis

4 (play) squash

5 swim

6 (do) aerobics

7 (buy) sports equipment

READING

3 Read the texts and say what these people like doing in their spare time.

Picture 1 – He likes . . .

1

People write to me from all over the world. I take these off envelopes and put them in my book. I've got a lot from France.

2

I listen to the BBC world service every day, and I repeat what they say. After the programme, I learn the new words.

3

We usually play at home but sometimes our friends ask us to play at parties. We want to be famous one day.

4

Some people think it's boring, but it isn't. I sit and think, and I often catch something and cook it for dinner.

WRITING: A letter

4 Read the advertisement below for activity holidays. Write a short letter to the company.

PARAGRAPH 1
Say what you like doing in your spare time.

PARAGRAPH 2
Ask them to send a brochure as soon as possible.

Don't forget to put in the letter:

- your address and the date
- the address of the company
- *Dear Sir / Madam*
- *Yours faithfully*

ACTIVITY HOLIDAYS FOR ALL AGES

For more information and a brochure write to:

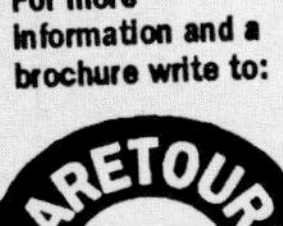

27 BRIDGE ST, EDINBURGH EH4 7HL

☆ Walking, climbing, riding, fishing
☆ Guitar and piano classes
☆ Painting, photography and film-making

All in a residential centre set in the beautiful mountains of Scotland. Seven and fourteen days.

Summary

FUNCTIONAL LANGUAGE

Talking about likes and dislikes
She likes tennis.
She likes playing tennis.
I don't like painting.
Do you like dancing?

Talking about present activities
She's listening to music.

GRAMMAR

The verb *to like*
like + noun
I like badminton.

like + *-ing*
They like playing golf.
He doesn't like gardening.
They don't like climbing.
Do you like climbing?

Present progressive tense

AFFIRMATIVE

FULL FORM	SHORT FORM
I am eating etc.	I'm eating etc.

NEGATIVE

FULL FORM	SHORT FORM
I am not eating etc.	I'm not eating etc.

INTERROGATIVE	SHORT ANSWERS
am I eating? etc.	Yes, I am. / No, I'm not. etc.

Question words
Why?
Why not?
What kind of . . . ?

Preposition
for eighteen hours

See the Grammar Reference section at the back of the book for more information.

Progress check 3

Vocabulary

1 Do people wear these clothes above the waist (A) or below the waist (B)? Make two lists.

A *B*
a sweater *socks*

socks a sweater tights shoes a jacket jeans a T-shirt

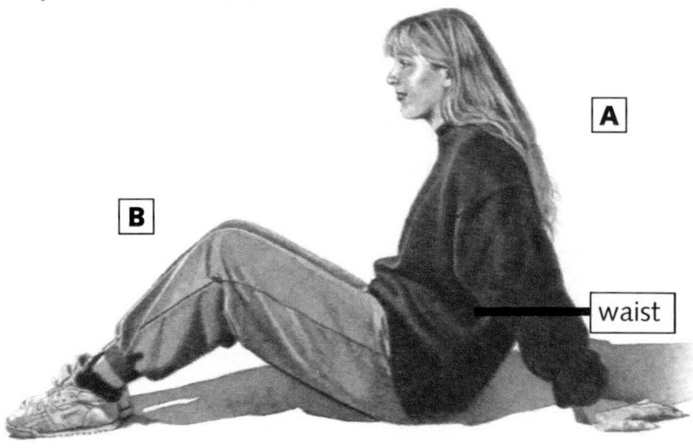

2 Match the shops with the things you buy there.

butcher's – meat

1 butcher's	fruit and vegetables
2 chemist's	stamps
3 baker's	newspapers and magazines
4 greengrocer's	meat
5 newsagent's	bread and cakes
6 post office	shampoo and soap

3 Write the times.

6.10 – *ten past six*

1 8.15 3 9.30 5 12.50
2 4.45 4 11.00 6 1.25

4 Write the days of the week in the correct order.

Monday, ...

5 Reorder the letters to make adjectives that describe hobbies.

g e s o n d u r a – dangerous

1 g r i n b o 4 l e x i n a r g
2 c l u f f i d i t 5 t i x i g e n c
3 a r e v i t e c 6 s t r e n g i n i t e

6 Look at the list of activities below. Find:

1 four sports that you play with a ball.
2 three sports that you play with a racquet.
3 two activities in water.
4 two activities that make a picture.
5 four other activities, not in 1–4.

1 tennis, ...

fishing aerobics photography tennis reading squash swimming painting badminton volleyball American football gardening running

Grammar and functions

7 Look at the picture and complete the conversation.

ASSISTANT: Can I help you?
CUSTOMER: Yes. I'd (1) ..... a plant, please.
ASSISTANT: (2) ..... one would you like?
CUSTOMER: (3) ..... big one, please.
ASSISTANT: Certainly. Anything else?
CUSTOMER: Yes. Can I (4) ..... some flowers?
ASSISTANT: (5) ..... roses are nice. How (6) ..... would you like?
CUSTOMER: Six, please. How (7) ..... is that?
ASSISTANT: Er – seventeen pounds, please.

8 **John is a shopkeeper. Look at the times he starts and finishes work. Then complete the sentences below with *sometimes, always, usually* or *never*.**

OPENING TIMES

Monday	9.00–5.00
Tuesday	9.00–5.00
Wednesday	9.00–5.00
Thursday	9.00–5.00
Friday	9.00–8.00
Saturday	9.00–12.00
Sunday	Closed

1 He ..... starts work at nine o'clock.
2 He ..... finishes work at five.
3 He ..... finishes work at eight.
4 He ..... works on Sundays.
5 He ..... finishes before five.

9 **John is talking about his week. Complete the sentences with *in, at, on* or *by*.**

'I have breakfast (1) ..... home, and then I go to work (2) ..... car. I start work (3) ..... nine o'clock (4) ..... the morning and usually finish (5) ..... about five (6) ..... the evening. I work six days a week, but (7) ..... Saturdays I finish at midday.'

10 **Complete the questions with *how much* or *how many*.**

1 ..... homework have we got?
2 ..... juice do you want?
3 ..... sports do you play?
4 ..... shampoo is there?
5 ..... evening classes do you do?
6 ..... hours is your flight to Mexico?

11 **Write questions or sentences with *like*.**

? you/read
Do you like reading?

1 ✗ she/swim
2 ? they/ride
3 ✓ he/write
4 ? you/cook
5 ✗ they/climb
6 ? she/study
7 ✓ we/dance
8 ✗ I/work

12 **Write questions about some of the people in Exercise 11. Ask about their activities now. Use the same verb.**

you/read?
Are you reading?

1 she/swim?
2 they/ride?
3 he/write?
4 you/cook?
5 they/climb?
6 she/study?

13 **What's Paul doing? Write the answers.**

It's six o'clock on Monday.
He's playing badminton.

1 It's eight o'clock on Tuesday.
2 It's half past six on Wednesday.
3 It's eight o'clock on Thursday.
4 It's ten o'clock on Friday.
5 It's eleven o'clock on Saturday morning.
6 It's twelve o'clock on Sunday morning.

Common errors

14 **Correct the mistakes.**

I am not like fishing.
I do not like fishing.

1 I like a cup of tea, please.
2 What time it is?
3 Is three o'clock.
4 Always he wears a suit to work.
5 How much cakes do you want?
6 They're listening music.

15 **Steffi wants information about language courses. Find five mistakes and correct them.**

Send me information about dates and fees.
Please send me information about dates and fees.

Tenby College
Tenby
Hants

Steffi Richter
73 River Street
Twyford
Hants SO21 8DL

Dear Tenby College
Send me information about dates and fees.

with love,
Steffi

At the end of the Progress Check, look back at your mistakes and study the Grammar Reference section if you need more help.

10 At the office

Abilities

Focus

- Talking about abilities
- Modal: *can/can't*
- Object pronouns: *me, you,* etc.
- Adverbs of degree

1 Describe Picture 1. Then listen and read. Are these sentences true or false?

1 James and Julia are working.
2 Rita is in the office.
3 James can type.
4 There isn't a word processor in the office.
5 James can use a word processor.

James and Julia are in the office.

JAMES: Where's Rita?
JULIA: James, it's half past six!
JAMES: Oh, yes.
JULIA: What did you want?
JAMES: Well, I wanted Rita to – well, I want to type a letter.
JULIA: Can you type?
JAMES: Yes – and no. Two fingers.
JULIA: Well, there's a word processor on Rita's desk. Can you use a word processor?
JAMES: Yes, yes ... well, I think so.

2 Listen to and read the rest of the conversation. What's James's problem now?

JAMES: Julia. There isn't a dollar sign.
JULIA: Yes, there is.
JAMES: I can't see it.
JULIA: Oh, James. What's that?
JAMES: Oh. Sorry. Thanks.

3 Pronunciation. Listen and repeat the words. Notice the underlined vowel sounds.

1 /ə/finger 2 /æ/thanks 3 /ɑː/car park.

Now listen and repeat these sentences. Match the vowel sounds 1–3 with *can* and *can't*.

Can he type? – 1

a) Can he type?
b) No, he can't.
c) Can she speak French?
d) Yes, she can.
e) They can't come.
f) I can come!

Listen again. Which words are stressed? What rules can you make about *can* and *can't*?

4 **Look at the pictures. Ask and answer.**

A: Can you type?

B: Yes, I can./Yes, a little./Yes, very well.

B: No, I can't./No, not at all.

1 type

2 drive

3 sing

4 draw

5 use a word processor

6 play an instrument

7 speak French

8 cook

5 **Ask your partner about other abilities. Then tell the class about your partner.**

He can play tennis very well.
He can speak German a little.
He can't ride at all.

6 **Work with a partner. Use the words and phrases below to say what you think healthy children can and can't do at different ages. Use a dictionary to help you.**

At birth babies can cry, but they can't crawl. At six months ...

walk talk in sentences crawl read cry kick a ball
hold something use a knife and fork drink from a cup

DISCOVERING LANGUAGE

7 **What do the words in bold print (object pronouns) refer to?**

There's a problem with the word processor. Can you look at **it**?
it = the word processor

1 These are important documents. Can you type **them**, please?
2 Here's Susan Warren's number. Can you phone **her**, please?
3 Is Mr Black in his office? I'd like to see **him**.
4 Julia, I can't type very well. Can you help **me**?
5 Rita – James and I would like to see Tom. Can you tell **us** when he's free?
6 James, can I phone **you** this evening?

8 **Complete the sentences with object pronouns.**

1 I'm in my office. Tell ..... when Mr Black arrives.
2 This way, Mr Black. Mr Hall can see ..... now.
3 We're at the station. Can you meet ..... here?
4 That's a photo of my sister. I'd like to see ..... on Saturday.
5 Where's my bag? Can you see .....?
6 This is my mother with my father. I always visit ..... in the summer.
7 Has Tom got the Beta Clocks video? Can you ask ....., please?

Working days

COMPARING CULTURES

1 Look at the signs and listen. Match the places with the signs below.

a bank – Sign 2

a department store	a small supermarket
a government office	a bank
a private company	a museum

1

Monday	9.30–6.00
Tuesday	9.30–6.00
Wednesday	9.30–6.00
Thursday	9.30–8.00
Friday	9.30–6.00
Saturday	9.30–6.00
Sunday	Closed

2

OPEN
MONDAY–FRIDAY
9.30–3.30

3

OPEN
7 DAYS
A WEEK
8 to 8

4

WORKING HOURS
9.00–5.30

5

OPENING HOURS
MON.–SAT.
10 a.m.–5 p.m.
SUN.
2.30 p.m.–6 p.m.

6

Open to the public
9.00-5.00
Monday to Friday

Focus

- Working hours/lives
- Further practice: buildings, routines, times

- Prepositions: *between, from, to* + times
- Adverbial phrase: *five days a week*
- Further practice: modal *can*, present simple tense, object pronouns

2 Now talk about the opening times.

The bank is open ***between*** *half past nine* ***and*** *half past three on Monday to Friday./The bank is open* ***from*** *nine thirty* ***to*** *three thirty, Monday to Friday.*

3 Compare working and opening hours in your country to those in Britain.

In Britain, people in offices work five days a week. In my country they work five and a half days a week.

4 Look at the pictures of the people in the magazine article and guess the answers to the questions.

1 What do these people do?
2 Where do they work?
3 Which days do they work?
4 What are their working hours?

Now read the articles and check your answers.

A DAY IN THE LIFE

Sally Oliver meets two people with very different lifestyles

JENNY

"My day starts at 6.30 a.m. I get up and go running before breakfast. I only have a small breakfast. I can't eat much in the morning – just a piece of toast with a cup of coffee. At half past seven I catch a train and I get to work at eight thirty.

I'm a sound engineer in a recording studio. I work five days a week, Monday to Friday.

When I arrive at the studio I look at the timetable. We record music and radio programmes, and sometimes advertisements. I go into the studio and prepare the equipment – the tape

IAN

"I'm an inventor. My job is to invent new things, and I work when I've got an idea. My studio is in my house, so I can work when I want to. Sometimes I work seven days a week; sometimes I don't work for days. I do all my creative work here, but I leave the house to go to meetings.

recorders and the mixing desk. I switch them on and make sure there are no problems. When the actors or musicians arrive, I give them microphones and check the sound. Then we start to record. I'm busy all day, but I usually have a break for a sandwich in the studio at one o'clock and I leave the studio at five. My job is quite difficult, but I like it. I play the saxophone in a band after work, so I like working with musicians.

–20

–25

I usually get up at about five o'clock. I make some tea, and start work at six. I drink tea all day – I can't work without it – but I don't eat anything until the evening.

First I tidy the studio. I switch on the answerphone because I can't speak to people when I've got an idea. Then I start work. I usually have a break after two or three hours, but I don't leave the studio. I do something different to help me relax. I often practise juggling. I can juggle well – it's an easy way to stop thinking about work problems. At other times I put some music on and play the drums. I play them for about an hour every day. I usually stop work at about nine o'clock in the evening. I think about my work most of the time, even when I'm out. I'm interested in what's around me and I like looking for new ideas, new problems to solve. For relaxation I play the drums in a blues band.

I'm working on a new kind of picture frame at the moment. It's a soft frame with elastic edges and plastic corners, and you can stretch it over any picture. It's a simple idea, but I think it's a good one.

–10 –15 –20 –25 –30 –35

5 Are these sentences true or false? Correct the false ones.

1 Jenny has a big breakfast.
2 She doesn't work on Saturday.
3 She goes home for lunch at one o'clock.
4 Ian works at home.
5 He has a sandwich at lunch-time.
6 He stops work in the afternoon.
7 His latest invention is a new kind of picture.

6 Describe the differences between Jenny's and Ian's lives.

Ian works at home. Jenny doesn't.
Jenny can play the saxophone. Ian can't.

7 Who or what do these words refer to in the articles?

ARTICLE 1
them (line 17) = *the tape recorders and the mixing desk*

ARTICLE 1
1 them (line 19)
2 it (line 24)

ARTICLE 2
1 it (line 11)
2 them (line 22)
3 it (line 33)

8 Work with a partner and a dictionary. How many nouns can you think of to replace the words in bold print?

We record **music**.
advertisements, programmes, songs

1 I catch **a train** to work.
2 I switch on **the tape recorder**.
3 I have **a break** at one o'clock.
4 I make **tea**.
5 I go to **work** at about seven thirty.

9 Write about your working day. Organise your writing like this.

PARAGRAPH 1
What time do you get up?
Where do you work/study and how do you travel?
What time do you start?

PARAGRAPH 2
What are the first things you do at work/college?
What do you do then?
When do you have a break?
When do you go home?

Development

SPEAKING

1 Look at Pictures 1–4. What can you say about them? Answer the questions.

1 Who are the people? Describe them.
2 Where are they? Describe the rooms they are in.
3 What are they doing?

LISTENING

2 Listen to the sounds. Match the equipment below with the sounds.

Sound 1 – I think it's a radio.

word processor air conditioner fax machine
video recorder photocopier coffee machine
answerphone radio

3 Listen to Mary-Lou Hoebee, the manager of a business centre in London. Which of these things are there in the centre?

telephones radios video recorders
photocopiers televisions fax machines
typewriters word processors air conditioners

4 Listen again and name the rooms where:

1 you can make coffee
2 you can sit and watch television
3 visitors can sit and wait

5 Listen again. The business centre offers a wide variety of services. Number the services in the order you hear them.

type letters – 1

order couriers prepare documents type letters
organise airline tickets order taxis

6 Receptionists at business centres take messages for clients. Listen to the conversation and read the message for Ms Daniels. Is it correct?

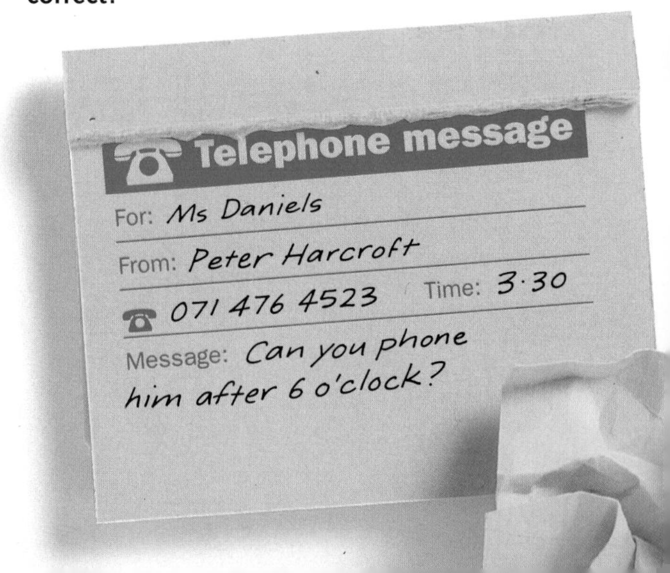

Telephone message

For: Ms Daniels

From: Peter Harcroft

☎ 071 476 4523 Time: 3·30

Message: Can you phone him after 6 o'clock?

WRITING

7 **Listen to a different conversation. Write a message to Ms Daniels.**

READING

8 **Read the text and answer the questions.**

"I'd like to be a pilot because it's an important, exciting job.

I can't fly a plane, but I can drive a car very well. I can speak English and I understand mechanical problems.

I like travelling and I also like working with computers."

1 What would you like to be? Give a reason.
2 Have you got the abilities?
3 Why would you like this job?

WRITING

9 **Write answers to the questions about a job you would like to have. Then exchange your writing with your partner. Check your partner's grammar, spelling and punctuation.**

Ask your partner for more information.

Why do you like travelling?
Is a pilot's job dangerous?
Does a pilot earn a good salary?

Answer your partner's questions. Make changes to your writing to improve it.

Summary

FUNCTIONAL LANGUAGE

Talking about abilities
He can speak French very well.
She can play the guitar a little.
He can't sing at all.
Can you type?
Yes, I can./No, I can't.

Talking about working hours
People in offices work five days a week.

GRAMMAR

Modal: *can/can't*

AFFIRMATIVE
I/you/he/she/it/we/they can type.

NEGATIVE
I/you/he/she/it/we/they can't type.

INTERROGATIVE
Can I/you/he/she/it/we/they type?

SHORT ANSWERS
Yes, I/you/he/she/it/we/they can.
No, I/you/he/she/it/we/they can't.

Object pronouns
me
you
him
her
it
us
them

Adverbs of degree
very well
a little
not at all

Adverbial phrase
five days a week

Prepositions
between nine and five
from nine thirty *to* three thirty

See the Grammar Reference section at the back of the book for more information.

11 Now and then

Focus

- The weather
- Temperatures
- Holidays

- Talking about past experiences
- Further practice: giving opinions

- Verb *to be*: past simple tense: affirmative, interrogative and short answers
- Adverbial phrases: *last week*, etc.

Holidays (1)

1 Listen and read. It is Rita's first day in the office after her holiday. Where was she?

JULIA: Rita! Hello!
RITA: Hello.
JULIA: How was your holiday?
RITA: Very nice, thank you.
JULIA: Where were you?
RITA: France. Near Bordeaux.
JULIA: Was the weather good?
RITA: The weather was wonderful.

2 Stress and intonation. Listen and repeat.

How was your holiday?

1 It was very nice.
2 It was wonderful.
3 It was lovely.
4 It was great.
5 It was OK.
6 It was all right.
7 It was terrible.
8 It was awful.
9 It wasn't very nice.

3 Listen again and match the answers with the expressions on the faces.

1 – A

4 Look at the pictures below. Ask and answer. Use adjectives from Exercise 2.

A: *How was the weather?*
B: *It was OK.*

5 Listen and compare the answers with your answers in Exercise 4. Then look at the list of adjectives below. Which adjectives do the speakers use to describe the weather in each picture?

Picture 1 – cold

wet cold cloudy warm sunny hot windy

Yesterday and last week

1 Listen to these people talking about where they, or their children, were yesterday. Make notes.

Truman: *at work*
Pauline's children: *at school*

Truman
Where were you yesterday?
Yesterday I was at work.

Pauline
Where were your children?
My children were at school yesterday.

1 Amanda
2 Mary-Lou
3 Sonia's daughter
4 Sonia's son
5 Shashi's son
6 Shashi's daughter
7 Mary-Lou's son

2 Check your answers to Exercise 1 with a partner.

A: *Was ... at work?*
B: *Yes, he/she was./No, he/she wasn't.*
A: *Were ... and ... at work?*
B: *Yes, they were./No, they weren't.*

3 Ask your partner where he/she was at the times below.

A: *Where were you yesterday morning?*
B: *I was at the shops.*

yesterday morning/afternoon/evening   last (Tuesday)
last week   last weekend   last (July)

4 Work in pairs. Talk about where Rosie and her friends were last week.

Student A: Look at the information on the map and complete part of the chart. Then ask and answer questions to complete the rest of the chart.
Student B: Look at the map on page 120. Answer and ask questions.

A: *Where was Mike?*
B: *He was in ...*
A: *How was the weather?*
B: *It was ...*
A: *What was the temperature?*
B: *It was ... degrees.*

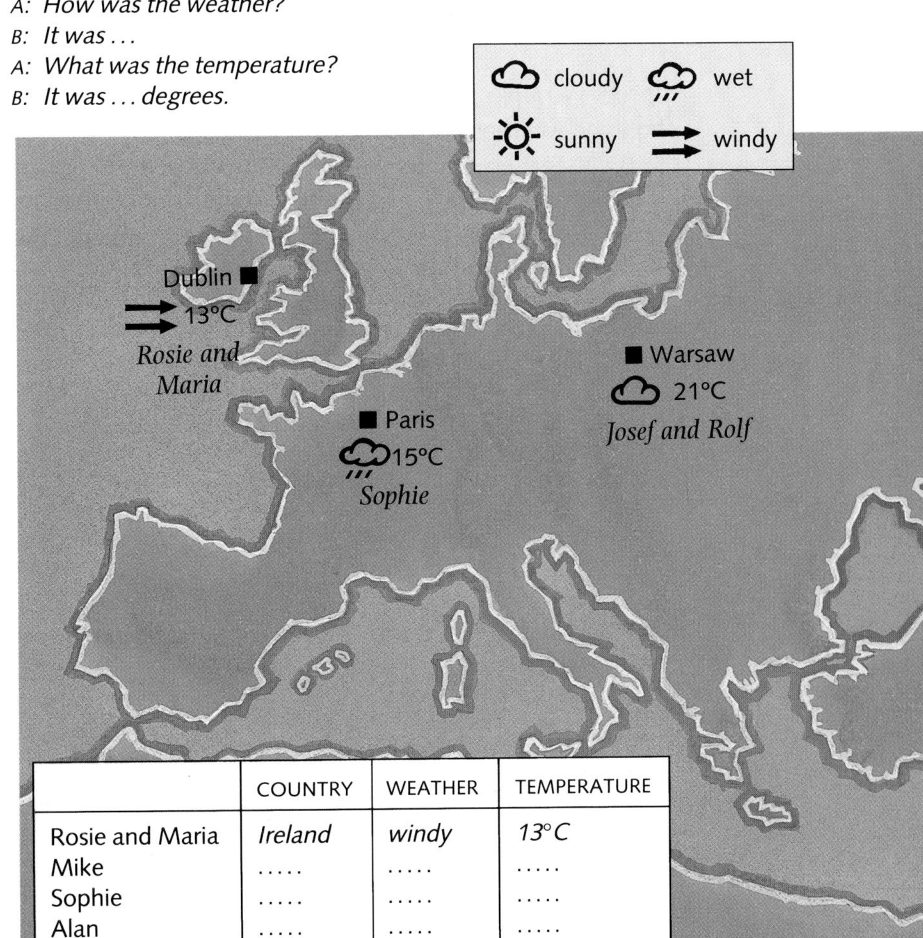

	COUNTRY	WEATHER	TEMPERATURE
Rosie and Maria	*Ireland*	*windy*	*13°C*
Mike	.....	.....	.....
Sophie	.....	.....	.....
Alan	.....	.....	.....
Josef and Rolf	.....	.....	.....
Poppy and John	.....	.....	.....

5 Read about Rosie and Maria.

Rosie and Maria were in Ireland last week. The weather was awful – it was cold and windy.

Now use information from the chart in Exercise 4 to write about:

1 Josef and Rolf   2 Alan

Focus

- Further practice: holidays
- Further practice: talking about the past, giving opinions
- Verb *to be*: past simple tense: negative
- Past simple tense: affirmative of regular verbs
- Further practice: verb *to be* past simple tense

Holidays (2)

1 [cassette symbol] Listen to the rest of the conversation about Rita's holiday. Are these sentences true or false?

1 It was wet every day.
2 Rita was in a hotel.
3 The food was awful.
4 She was with a friend.

RITA: One day (1) ..... terrible – it (2) ..... cold and wet, but the other days (3) ..... hot.
SANDRA: How (4) ..... your hotel?
RITA: We – I (5) ..... with my friend, Carol – we (6) .....n't in a hotel. We (7) ..... in a caravan. Very cheap.
JULIA: Mm. (8) ..... it nice?
RITA: Yes, it (9) ..... great.
SANDRA: How (10) ..... the food?
RITA: There (11) ..... some wonderful restaurants in the town. One (12) .....n't very good, but the others – mmm.

2 [cassette symbol] Listen again. Complete the conversation with *was* or *were*.

DISCOVERING LANGUAGE

3 What are the rules for the past simple tense of the verb *to be*? How do we make questions? How do we make negative statements?

Complete the chart with the forms of the past simple tense of the verb *to be*.

	AFFIRMATIVE	NEGATIVE	INTERROGATIVE
I	I was	.....	.....
you	.....	.....	.....
he/she/it	.....	she wasn't	.....
we	.....	.....	.....
they	.....	.....	were they?

4 Work in groups. Look at the topics and adjectives below. List the adjectives you can use to talk about each of the topics. Use a dictionary to help you.

TOPICS
weather hotel food

ADJECTIVES
clean friendly cloudy hot
salty cold great awful
warm oily bad sunny
expensive delicious good
wet terrible cheap dirty

5 Ask and answer. Use the topics and adjectives from Exercise 4 to talk about your last holiday.

A: *Where were you?*
B: *I was in Florida.*
A: *When were you there?*
B: *Last August.*
A: *How was the weather?*
B: *It was great – very hot.*
A: *How was the hotel?*
B: *It was OK. It was clean.*
A: *How was the food?*
B: *It was delicious.*

6 Now tell the class about your partner's holiday.

Birgit was in Florida last August. The weather was great. It was very hot. The hotel was OK. It was clean. The food was delicious.

7 Write a paragraph about your holiday.

Eldon House,
Windrush Road,
Brighton,
East Sussex BN2 6AE

30.9.93

Dear Katia,

I am back in Brighton now after a great holiday with Rosie in Dublin. I really enjoyed it.

We travelled by train and boat. I hated the boat journey - I tried to sleep, but it was very difficult. We were both very tired when we arrived, but her parents were wonderful. We stayed with them for two weeks and they cooked lovely meals for us. I practised my English all the time.

We visited Rosie's friends and also some of Dublin's beautiful buildings. The castle was closed so we didn't go in; we just looked at the outside. I liked the university very much. What a great place to be a student! (I'm enclosing a photo of Trinity College.) I also loved the pubs, with their music and friendly atmosphere. The weather was awful, it was very wet, but everything else was fantastic.

See you when you come back to Brighton.

Love,
Maria

8 **Read Maria's letter to her friend Katia about her holiday in Ireland. Find these verbs in the letter and write them in the past simple tense.**

stay practise visit look at try

9 **Find two verbs with a similar meaning to *like*.**

10 **Say what Maria liked.**

She liked the holiday in Dublin.

DISCOVERING LANGUAGE

11 **Find all the past simple tense verbs in the letter. Which of these rules does each verb follow?**

1. Infinitive + *ed*
   talk + *ed* = *talked*
2. Infinitive + *d*
   like + *d* = *liked*
3. Infinitive minus *y* + *ied*
   cry *cried*
4. Infinitive + double final consonant + *ed*
   stop *stopped*

12 **Pronunciation. Listen to the past simple tense verbs. Do they end in the sound /d/, /t/ or /ɪd/?**

played	talked	waited
visited	loved	liked
stayed	hated	travelled

Listen again and repeat.

ENGLISH AROUND YOU

Where were you yesterday?
I was at the zoo.

Places to visit

Focus

- Holiday locations
- Describing places
- Prepositions: *in* + place, *at* + place, *on* holiday
- Further practice: present simple tense, past simple tense

1 **Look at the pictures. In which countries can you find places like these? Are there places like them in your country?**

2 **Work with a partner. Which of the adjectives in the chart can describe the nouns below? Use a dictionary to help you.**

SIZE	DIMENSION	COLOUR	OTHERS
small big huge high tall	shallow deep	golden silver blue green yellow black grey	empty crowded quiet noisy

beach – small, . . .

1 beach 3 mountains 5 stream 7 lake 9 sand
2 sea 4 rocks 6 trees 8 dunes 10 sky

Can you think of any other adjectives for these nouns?

1 the forest
forest tree

2 the mountains
mountain snow rock stream lake

3 the seaside
beach sea boat

4 the desert
sand dune sky palm tree

3 Listen to three people talking about their favourite holiday places. Make notes about them in the chart.

	PLACE	COUNTRY	REASONS	USUAL TIME FOR HOLIDAY
Helen	*seaside*	.....	*lovely beaches* *shallow sea*	.....
Rob	.....	*United States*	....	.....
Jill	.....	.....	....	*March/April*

Now tell your partner about your favourite holiday place. Say why you like it and when you go.

4 **Write about a place that you would like to visit. Give reasons. Think about the weather, the countryside and things to do.**

I'd like to go to the mountains because I like climbing. It's exciting.

I wouldn't like to go to the seaside. The beaches are always crowded and noisy. It's often very hot, and I don't like sunbathing.

5 **Read the postcard once quickly. Choose the correct answer.**

Anna and Tim are on holiday:

a) in the desert c) at the seaside
b) in the forest d) in the mountains.

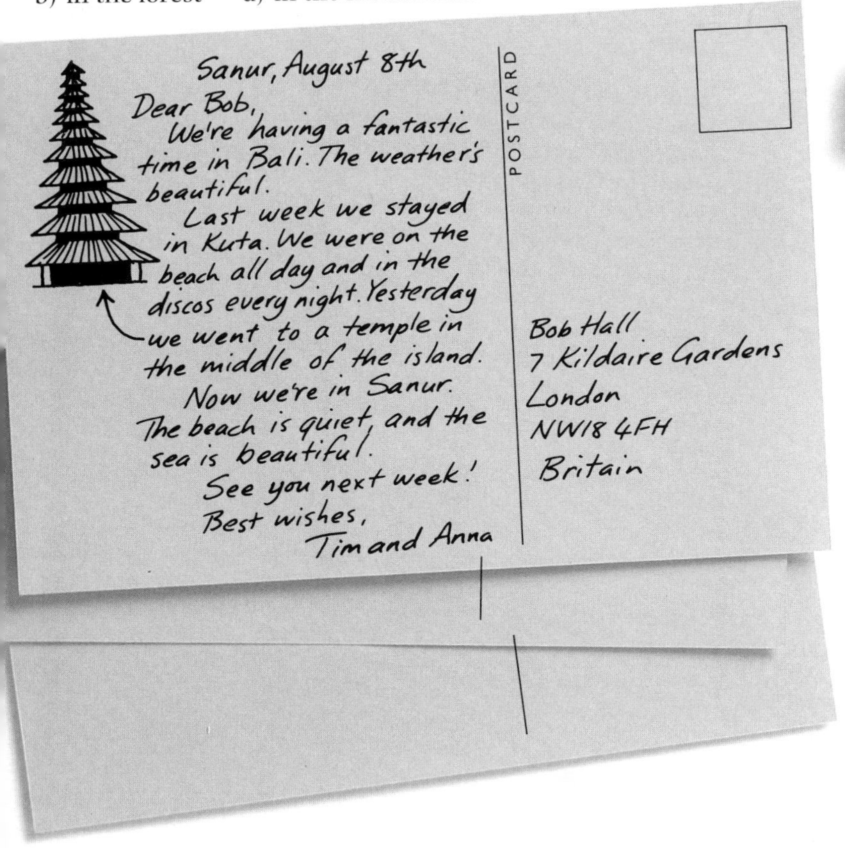

Sanur, August 8th

Dear Bob,
We're having a fantastic time in Bali. The weather's beautiful.
Last week we stayed in Kuta. We were on the beach all day and in the discos every night. Yesterday we went to a temple in the middle of the island.
Now we're in Sanur. The beach is quiet, and the sea is beautiful.
See you next week!
Best wishes,
Tim and Anna

POSTCARD

Bob Hall
7 Kildaire Gardens
London
NW18 4FH
Britain

NOTE: *went* is the irregular past simple tense form of the verb *go*.

6 **Read the postcard again. Say which paragraph (1, 2 or 3) contains the following information:**

1 the place they are staying in now
2 the weather
3 their past activities
4 their general feelings about their holiday

7 **Match these words with the times below.**

now next (Monday/week/month/year) last (Monday/week/month/year) yesterday

1 the past 3 the future
2 the present

COMPARING CULTURES

8 **There are different ways of ending an informal letter or postcard in English. Here are three of them.**

Love, John

Best wishes, Teresa

With all my love, Susie

Which of them do we use when we write to:

1 a girlfriend / boyfriend / wife / husband?
2 a friend or colleague?
3 a very good friend?

How do you end an informal letter or postcard to each of these people in your language?

9 **You are on holiday in one of the other places shown in Exercise 1 or in a place that you know. Write a postcard to a British friend. Organise your writing in the same way as in the postcard in Exercise 5.**

Development

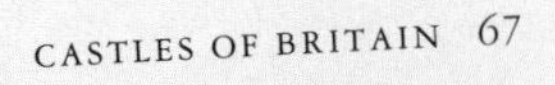

Leeds Castle

MAIDSTONE, KENT

A Norman baron built Leeds Castle in 1119, and his family lived there for about 160 years. It then became a royal palace and the home of six queens of England, including the Spanish princess, Eleanor of Castile. From 1552 the castle was the home of a governor of Ireland, and it remained a private home until 1976.

Today the castle is a museum and conference centre. Many of the rooms are the same as they were in the past, with old furniture and paintings. The King's Dining Room, more than twenty metres long, has furniture from the fifteenth and sixteenth centuries. The Queen's Room, which was a bedroom, a dining room and a reception room, is decorated as it was in 1430. The Queen's Bathroom has a wooden bath where the queen washed. The Great Hall is now a museum. All these rooms are open to the public. Some other rooms – the library and the billiard room, for example – are used for seminars and meetings. These rooms have modern furniture and equipment.

The castle and its beautiful gardens are open to the public all year round ■

SPEAKING

1 Look at the pictures in the guidebook to Leeds Castle. Work with a partner. Discuss these questions.

1 Where is the castle?
2 How old is it?
3 What kind of people lived there?
4 Who lives there now?
5 What rooms and furniture are inside?
6 The woman works in the castle. What's her job? What exactly does she do?
7 What do you think she is saying?

READING

2 Now read the text in the guidebook. Were your answers about the castle and furniture correct?

3 Match the sentences with the dates.

1 Leeds Castle was a royal palace.	1119
2 Leeds Castle became a museum and conference centre.	1552
3 A Norman baron built Leeds Castle.	1976
4 A governor of Ireland lived in Leeds Castle.	1279

LISTENING

4 Listen to Pat Carr, the woman in Picture 4. Answer the questions.

1 Were you right about her job? What is it?
2 Where do visitors to the castle come from?
3 Does she like her job? Why?/Why not?
4 Do you think Pat's job is a good job? Why?/Why not?

WRITING

5 Work with a partner. Write about a famous building that you know. Use the following questions to help you.

PARAGRAPH 1
Who built it? When? Why is it famous?

PARAGRAPH 2
What happened in it? What do people use it for now?

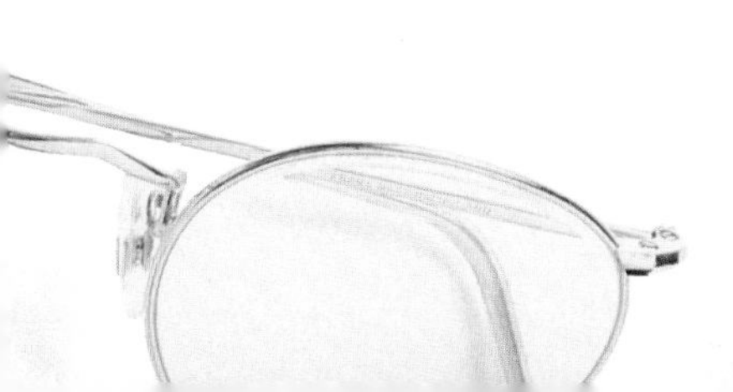

Summary

FUNCTIONAL LANGUAGE

Asking about past experiences
How was your holiday?

Giving opinions
It was wonderful/all right/awful.

Describing places
The beaches are always crowded and noisy.

Talking about the weather
It's/It was hot.
It's/It was twenty-nine degrees.

GRAMMAR

The verb *to be*: past simple tense

AFFIRMATIVE	NEGATIVE FULL FORM	NEGATIVE SHORT FORM
I was	I was not	I wasn't
you were	you were not	you weren't
he/she/it was	he was not	he wasn't
we were	we were not	we weren't
they were	they were not	they weren't

INTERROGATIVE	SHORT ANSWERS
was I?	Yes, I was./No, I wasn't.
were you?	Yes, you were./No, you weren't.
was he/she/it?	Yes, he/she/it was./ No, he/she/it wasn't.
were we?	Yes, we were./No, we weren't.
were they?	Yes, they were./No, they weren't.

The past simple tense: regular verbs
AFFIRMATIVE
I played
you played
he/she/it played
we played
they played

Adverbial phrases
now
next (week)
last (week)
yesterday

Prepositions
in the mountains/forest/desert
at the seaside
on holiday

Adjectives
It's beautiful.
It's a beautiful beach.
The beach is beautiful.

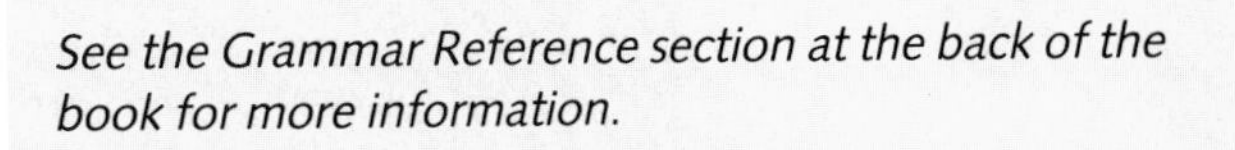
See the Grammar Reference section at the back of the book for more information.

12 When we were young

Focus

- Interviews
- Educational history
- Job history
- Years

- Talking about dates and places of birth
- Past simple tense: negative and interrogative of regular and irregular verbs
- Further practice: preposition: *in* + year

E.C. Passport
Passport No.
700318289
Name:
Napoleon
Bonaparte
Date of birth:
1769
Profession:
Soldier
Where were you born?
I was born in Corsica.
When?
In 1769.

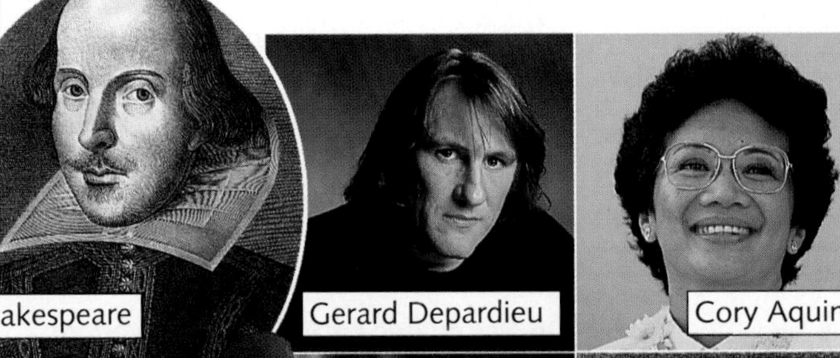

Interviews

1 **Listen and repeat the conversation on the left.**

2 **Say the dates.**

1919 *nineteen nineteen*
1400 *fourteen hundred*
1907 *nineteen-oh-seven*

1	1769	5	1918
2	1986	6	1869
3	1540	7	1705
4	1800	8	1997

3 **Match the people on the left with the countries and dates of birth below. Ask and answer.**

A: *Where was Napoleon born?*
B: *He was born in Corsica.*
A: *When was he born?*
B: *He was born in 1769.*

China France
the United States Italy
Argentina Britain
the Philippines Corsica

1451	1564	1889
1893	1933	1948
1769	1961	1970

4 **Ask and answer about your partner and his/her family.**

Where/When were you born?
Where/When was your (father) born?

5 **Tell the class about your partner.**

Marketing
Advertising
Publicity

APPLICATION FORM

First name	(1) .....
Surname	(2) .....
Date of birth	(3) .....
Place of birth	(4) .....
Education	*Fendale Secondary School* (5) ..... *Business College*
Qualifications	(6) ..... *in Marketing*
Other work	*Marketing Assistant with* (7) ..... *Group in Liverpool: Oct '92 to* (8) .....

6 Tom Hall is interviewing a woman for a job at MAP Advertising. Listen and complete her application form.

7 Now read the interview and check your answers.

TOM: Right. Your surname is Peters. P-E-T-E-R-S?
SARAH: That's right. Sarah Peters.
TOM: And when were you born, Ms Peters?
SARAH: January 4th, 1973.
TOM: OK. Tell me a little bit about yourself.
SARAH: Well, I was born in Brighton and I lived there until I was ten. Then we moved to Oxford.
TOM: Did you stay in Oxford for long?
SARAH: Yes, I did. I stayed there until I left school – that's Fendale Secondary School – at eighteen. Then I went to college.
TOM: Which college did you go to?
SARAH: The London Business College, and I got a Diploma in Marketing there.
TOM: A Diploma in Marketing. And after that? What did you do next? Did you stay in London?
SARAH: No, I didn't. I got a job with a hotel group – the TFC Hotel Group – in Liverpool, as a marketing assistant. That was in October 1992. I left there in October 1993.
TOM: I see. And why did you leave?
SARAH: I didn't want to stay in Liverpool. I wanted to work in London.

DISCOVERING LANGUAGE

8 Read the interview again and list the regular and irregular past simple tense affirmative forms.

REGULAR: *lived, . . .* IRREGULAR: *went, . . .*

Now complete the chart with the past simple tense forms of *live* and *go*.

	REGULAR	IRREGULAR
Affirmative	.....	.....
Negative	.....	*didn't go*
Interrogative	.....	.....

9 Pronunciation. Listen to the /dʒ/ sound in these questions.

Where did you go? What did you say?
Who did you see?

Listen again and repeat.

Now say these questions. Then listen and compare your pronunciation with the cassette.

When did you come? Who did you meet?
How did you travel?

10 Work in pairs.

Student A: Ask more questions about Sarah.
Student B: Turn to page 121 and read another version of Sarah's interview with Tom. Then answer your partner's questions.

why/move to Oxford?
A: *Why did Sarah move to Oxford?*
B: *Because . . .*

1 why/move to Oxford?
2 what/study at school?
3 why/study marketing?
4 when/finish college?
5 work/in a hotel?
6 like/job?

11 Ask and answer about when you and your partner were children. Note your partner's answers. Ask as many questions as you can.

Where did you go to school?
When did you start/leave?
Did you like it? Why/why not?
Did you go to college?
What did you study?

12 Now tell the class about your partner.

Interesting lives

Writer at 16

Drummer plays on

Focus

- Biographies
- Conjunctions: *before, after, until, when*
- Adverbs: *then, later, at first*
- Further practice: past simple tense: all forms

1

CAROLL SPINNEY, now fifty-seven, started working with puppets when he was eight years old. In 1969 he started work on *Sesame Street*, an American television series for children. Today, the series is shown on television in more than eighty countries and Spinney is still the man inside an eight-foot yellow chicken called Big Bird.

Spinney loves his work and knows that he has a responsibility to children watching the programme. He doesn't want children to know that Big Bird is really a man, so he tries to be very careful. Once, though, a child saw him as he climbed out of his costume. She looked at him and then said, 'Mommy! Does Big Bird know he's got a man inside him?'

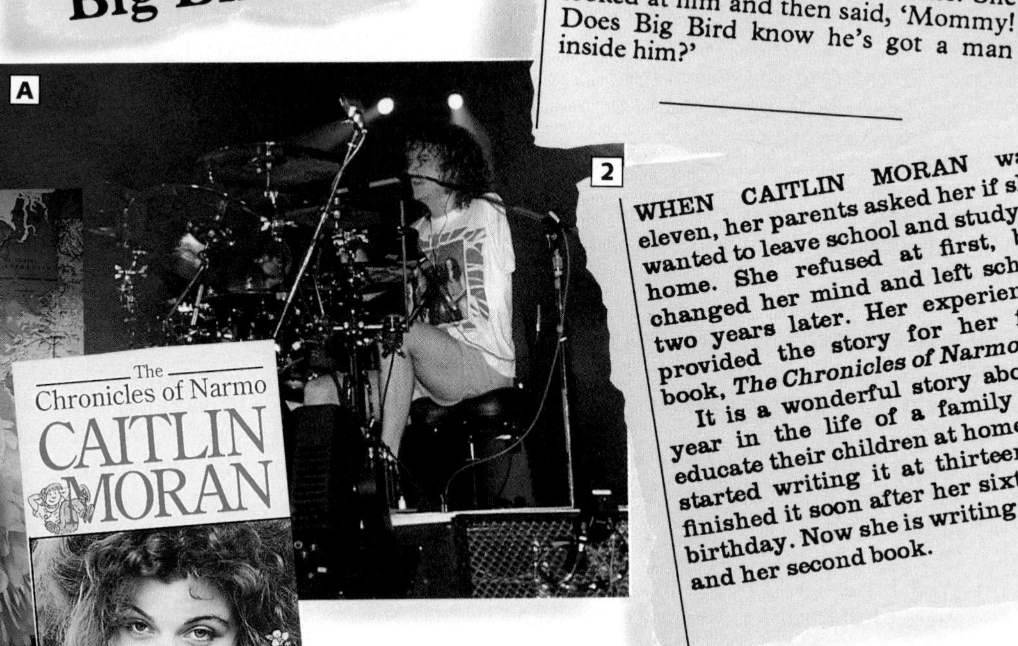

2

WHEN CAITLIN MORAN was eleven, her parents asked her if she wanted to leave school and study at home. She refused at first, but changed her mind and left school two years later. Her experiences provided the story for her first book, *The Chronicles of Narmo.*

It is a wonderful story about a year in the life of a family who educate their children at home. She started writing it at thirteen an finished it soon after her sixteent birthday. Now she is writing a pla and her second book.

1 **Describe the photographs. What do you think the newspaper articles are about?**

2 **Look at the headlines. Match them with the photographs and the articles.**

3 **Work in groups of three. Choose one article each and read the first paragraph. Then tell people in your group what the article is about.**

4 **Read all the articles quickly. Look for the answers to the questions below and then check your answers with a partner. Which person (Caroll, Rick or Caitlin) . . .**

1 . . . is a musician?
2 . . . is a writer?
3 . . . is an actor?
4 . . . has a famous costume?
5 . . . has a famous face?
6 . . . is under twenty years old?
7 . . . is over fifty years old?
8 . . . had lessons at home?
9 . . . is in a television series?
10 . . . works alone?
11 . . . works in a small group?
12 . . . works with a lot of other people?

3

Rick Allen, the well-known drummer with the Irish rock band Def Leppard, joined the band on his fifteenth birthday after playing the drums for six years. A year later, in 1979, the band became famous. Then, in 1984, Rick had a very bad car accident and lost his left arm.

His life changed in many ways, but he realised that his feet could do a lot of the work of his left arm, and a friend developed an electronic drum kit so that he could play the drums with an arm and two feet. He returned to the band and he still performs with them now. The first time he played in a big concert everybody was so kind that he cried. He was worried about water in the electronic system below him!

Now Rick is married and has a home life. Life with one arm is still a problem, but if he can't chop vegetables with one hand he simply uses his feet.

5 Write the past simple tense forms of these verbs. Check with the articles. Guess the meaning of new words. Then check with your dictionary.

ARTICLE 1
start climb see say

ARTICLE 2
ask provide refuse finish

ARTICLE 3
join lose can become change develop have realise return

6 Correct the sentences.

Rick Allen played the guitar for six years before he joined Def Leppard.
He didn't play the guitar. He played the drums.

1 Caroll Spinney worked with birds when he was eight years old.
2 He left Sesame Street in 1969.
3 Rick Allen lost his right arm in 1984.
4 He joined a new band after his accident.
5 Caitlin Moran went to a new school when she was thirteen.
6 She finished her first book when she was fifteen.

7 Read the sentences. Which event or situation in each sentence was first (1) and which event was second (2)? (If the times are the same, write no numbers.)

At first Caitlin refused [1] to leave school, but later she changed [2] her mind.

1 When Rick Allen was fifteen, he joined Def Leppard.
2 Before he lost his left arm, Rick played with a normal drum kit.
3 He used both arms in those days; now he uses one arm and both feet.
4 Caitlin Moran wrote *The Chronicles of Narmo*, and then started writing a play and a second book.
5 Caroll Spinney got a job with *Sesame Street* after he worked with puppets as a child and young man.
6 Rick couldn't play the drums with one arm until a friend developed an electronic drum kit.

8 Complete the sentences with these words:

at first when after then/later before now until

1 Caitlin started writing her first book ..... she was thirteen.
2 She stayed at school ..... she was thirteen.
3 She finished her first book just ..... her sixteenth birthday.
4 Rick lost his arm. ..... it was difficult to play the drums, but ..... he learnt to play in a different way.
5 ..... he has got a special drum kit.
6 Caroll was Big Bird ..... *Sesame Street* became famous around the world.

9 Make notes about an interesting person that you know about. Then tell the class.

ENGLISH AROUND YOU

Development

SPEAKING

1 The photographs above tell us something about the life of an American woman called Billie Schacht. Look at them and answer the questions.

1 Describe the pictures. How old do you think they are?
2 Who do you think the people in the photos are?

READING AND LISTENING

2 Read the summary of an interview with Billie Schacht. Discuss possible ways to complete it. Then listen and complete it.

Billie Schacht was born in Minnesota, USA in the year (1) ...... She and her parents lived on a (2) ..... in the country. She went to (3) ..... in Millville, a town near her home. One teacher taught all the subjects to one class of children between the ages of (4) ..... and (5) ......

There were four possible occupations for women in those days: to become a nurse, a (6) ..... or a (7) ....., or to get married. Billie decided to be a (8) ...... She liked the job very much indeed.

SPEAKING

3 Tell your partner about your experiences at primary school. Talk about: the number of people in the school/in your class; the teachers; your friends; travelling to school.

There were two hundred children at my primary school. ...

Do you think your partner's school was a good school? Why?/Why not?

USEFUL PAST SIMPLE TENSE FORMS	
learn – learnt	teach – taught

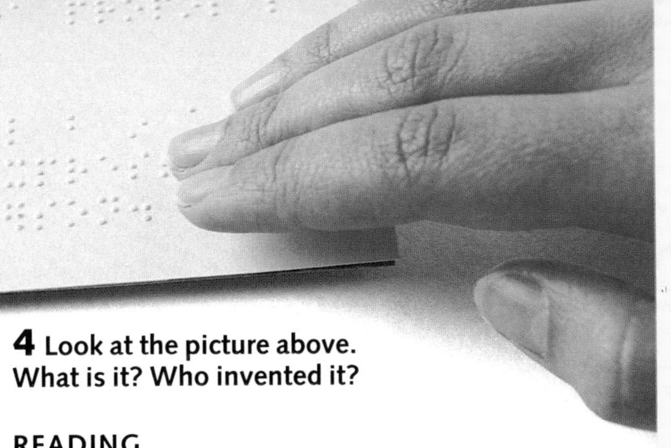

4 **Look at the picture above. What is it? Who invented it?**

READING

5 **Read this information about the inventor of the Braille writing system.**

NAME: Louis Braille YEAR OF BIRTH: 1809
PLACE OF BIRTH: Paris, France

1812 Had an accident in his father's workshop and went blind
1819 Started school at the National Institute for Blind Children in Paris
1824 Developed a system of writing based on dots
1826 Became a teacher at the Institute
1852 Died of tuberculosis
1854 French National Institute started using Braille system
1932 Braille was introduced as the writing system for the blind in the English-speaking world

WRITING: A biography

6 **Now correct and rewrite this short biography.**

Louis Braille was born in Germany in 1812. When he was five, he had an accident and went blind. He started school at the National Institute for Deaf Children at the age of 10. Then in 1825 he developed his own writing system for the blind. Two years later he started work at the Institute as a teacher, and he taught there until he died in 1952.

The National Institute in Paris did not use the Braille system, but in 1932 every country in the world introduced it as an international writing system for the blind.

7 **Interview a friend or a member of your family. Then write a short biography of that person.**

Summary

FUNCTIONAL LANGUAGE

Talking about dates and places of birth
When were you born?
In 1970.
Where were you born?
In Buenos Aires.

Saying when something happened
When I was a child, we lived in London.
We lived there until I was fifteen.
Then we moved to a small town.
At first I liked it, but later I moved again.
Before 1985 I was a student.
After 1985 I worked in a computer company.
Five years later I became a company director.

Warning someone
Be careful!

GRAMMAR

Past simple tense: regular verbs

AFFIRMATIVE
I/you/he/she/it/we/they played

NEGATIVE
I/you/he/she/it/we/they did not/didn't play

INTERROGATIVE
did I/you/he/she/it/we/they play?

SHORT ANSWERS
Yes, I/you/he/she/it/we/they did.
No, I/you/he/she/it/we/they didn't.

Past simple tense: irregular verbs
Example: *go*

AFFIRMATIVE	she went
NEGATIVE	she did not/didn't go
INTERROGATIVE	did she go?
SHORT ANSWERS	Yes, she did./No, she didn't.

Conjunctions
before
after
until
when

Adverbs
then
later
at first

See the Grammar Reference section at the back of the book for more information.

Progress check 4

Vocabulary

1 Put the words below into two groups.

OFFICE EQUIPMENT MUSICAL INSTRUMENTS
telephone *saxophone*

telephone saxophone drums typewriter word processor fax air conditioner computer guitar answerphone piano photocopier

2 Put the words and phrases into three groups.

GOOD BAD NOT GOOD OR BAD
all right

OK fantastic lovely great terrible beautiful wonderful awful very nice all right I hated ... I loved ...

3 Complete the sentences. Use some of these words:

deep shallow tall high empty huge quiet crowded

1 You can walk across the river here. The water is very ..... .
2 I love going to the mountains in winter. There aren't any other people there. The roads are ..... and everything is ..... .
3 The mountains in the Himalayas are very ..... .
4 I hate beaches in the summer. They're always ..... .

4 Complete the sentences to describe the weather.

It's ..... and ..... .
It's warm and wet.

1 It's .....

2 It's ..... and ..... .

3 It's ..... and ..... .

Grammar and functions

5 What are the people in the pictures saying? Use *can* or *can't*.

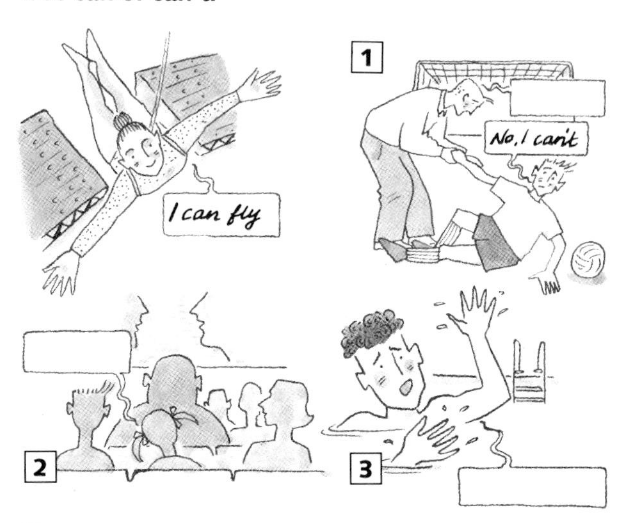

6 Look at this information about some of the things James can and can't do. Write a question and an answer for each one. Use one of these phrases: *very well, a little, (not) at all.*

drive a car 0 1 2 3 4 (5)
Can James drive a car?
Yes, he can drive a car very well.

1 sing 0 1 2 3 4 (5)
2 use a word processor 0 (1) 2 3 4 5
3 speak Spanish (0) 1 2 3 4 5

7 Complete the text with *on, in, to* or *at*.

We went (1) ..... the USA (2) ..... holiday (3) ..... 1993. We spent a week (4) ..... the mountains and another week (5) ..... the seaside. Then we had a few days (6) ..... New York before we came home.

8 **Complete the sentences with these words:**

me him us it her them

1 Where's my bag? I can't see ......
2 Oh, isn't Sally there? Can you ask ..... to phone me?
3 My parents like the theatre. We can go with ......
4 Pat? Hello! Tom and I are in Birmingham. Can you meet ..... for lunch?
5 I don't understand this. Can you help ..... ?
6 That's Alan. Would you like to meet ..... ?

9 **Complete the postcard with four of these words and with the correct form of the verbs in brackets.**

now after when then great yesterday

5300 BONN am Rhein

Dear Sally,
We're having a (1) ______ time here. (2) ______ we (3) ______ (arrive) the weather (4) ______ (be) terrible, but it's lovely (5) ______ .
(6) ______ we (7) ______ (visit) a castle in the morning, and in the afternoon we (8) ______ (go) to the shops. In the evening we (9) ______ (have) dinner in a beautiful restaurant on the river.
(10) ______ (see) you soon.
Love Lucy

125 Jahre Galopprennbahn Hoppegarten
DEUTSCHE BUNDESPOST 80

Sally Hall
7 Kildaire Gardens
London
NW8 4FH
UK

10 **Tom is interviewing Anne for a job. Write his questions.**

TOM: (1) ....?
ANNE: I was born in the United States.
TOM: (2) ....?
ANNE: I went to primary school in the States and then my family moved to Britain, so I went to secondary school here.
TOM: (3) ....?
ANNE: Because my father got a new job in London.
TOM: (4) ....?
ANNE: I was twelve. When I left school, I went to university in Scotland – in Edinburgh.
TOM: (5) ....?
ANNE: Because I like Scotland, and I wanted to leave London.
TOM: (6) ....?
ANNE: I studied languages – French and Spanish.

11 **Write the past simple tense form of the verbs.**

enjoy – *enjoyed*

arrive stay cook travel live leave practise get visit go study have lose like love teach become see say

Common errors

12 **Choose the correct sentence, (a) or (b).**

a) I can't type. ✓
b) I don't can type.

1 a) I can cook very well.
  b) I can very well cook.
2 a) He can't paint at all.
  b) He can paint not at all.
3 a) They can't to swim.
  b) They can't swim.
4 a) Do you can drive?
  b) Can you drive?
5 a) When can she come?
  b) When she can come?

13 **Correct the mistakes.**

He were at university with me.
He was at university with me.

1 Was you here yesterday?
2 We goed out to dinner with friends.
3 Did she was late for class?
4 The teacher didn't taught us that!
5 Do you visit London last year?
6 Where you did see that film?

14 **Correct the answers to the questions. Add the missing word to each answer.**

'Where were you on Saturday?'
'I at my mother's house.'
I was at my mother's house.

1 'Do you like music?'
  'Yes, I like very much.'
2 'Where are you from?'
  'I born in Geneva.'
3 'What are you doing?'
  'I'm looking your homework.'
4 'What's the problem?'
  'Is a mistake in this exercise.'
5 'What did you do then?'
  'I became nurse.'

At the end of the Progress Check, look back at your mistakes and study the Grammar Reference section if you need more help.

13 Eating out

WE'RE HAVING A
PARTY!
John and Steve
invite Rosie to a party
on Saturday June 15th at 8 pm
RSVP Tel 772366

Invitations

Focus

- Further practice: spare-time activities, food

- Inviting
- Accepting
- Refusing
- Thanking
- Polite requests
- Talking about quantity
- Offering

- *Could you ... ?*
- *A lot (of), a few, a little, many, much*
- Adverbial phrases: *this evening, this weekend, tonight, tomorrow*
- Further practice: *would like* + infinitive

1 Listen and read.

1 ROSIE: Have you got any plans for this evening, Maria?
MARIA: No, I haven't. Why?
ROSIE: Would you like to come to dinner?
MARIA: I'd love to. Thanks.

2 MARCO: Teresa ... would you like to go out for a meal this evening?
TERESA: Sorry, Marco, I'm busy tonight.
MARCO: Oh, well. Another time perhaps.
TERESA: Yes. How about tomorrow?

2 Pronunciation. Listen to the sound /dʒ/ at the end of ***would*** and the beginning of ***you***.

Would you like to come to dinner?

Now listen and repeat.

Would you ... ? Would you like ... ?
Would you like to go out?
Would you like to go out for a meal this evening?

3 Invite your partner to the places in the pictures.

go out for a meal/weekend
A: *Would you like to go out for a meal this weekend?*
B: *I'd love to. Thanks./Sorry. I'd love to, but I'm busy.*

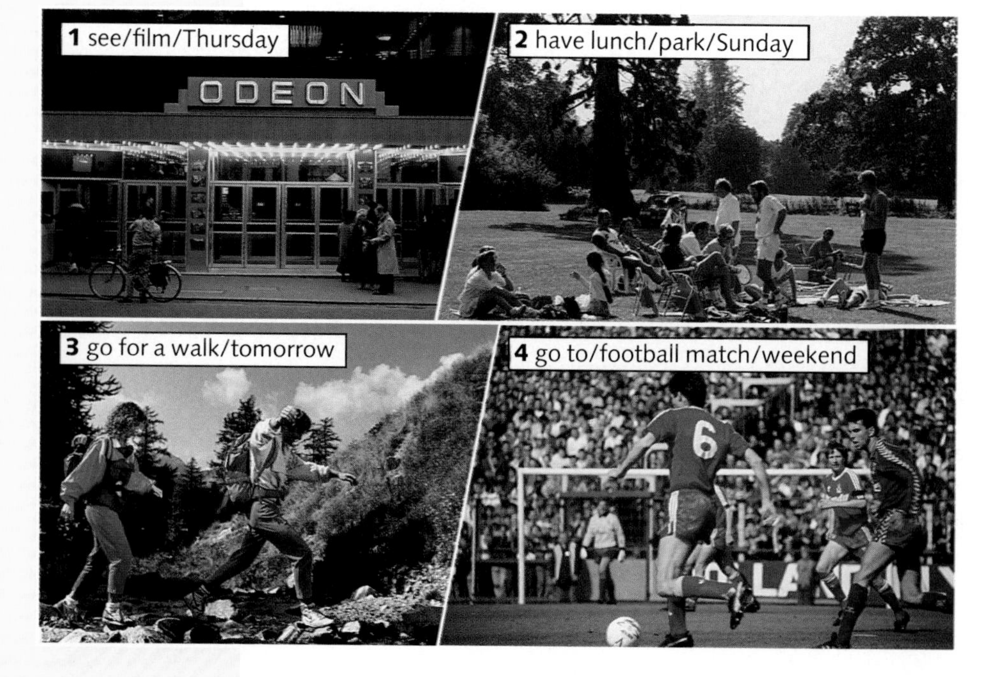

4 Look at the invitation and at Rosie's reply. Answer the questions.

1 When is the party?
2 Can Rosie go? Why?/Why not?
3 What do you think 'RSVP' means?

Flat 4
37 Egremont Rd
Brighton
BN3 2WR
December 3rd

Dear John and Steve
Thank you very much for inviting me to your party.
I'm afraid that I can't come because I'm busy on Saturday.
I hope you have a lovely party.
Best wishes,
Rosie

5 Look at Rosie's letter again and answer the questions.

1 After her address and the date, how does she start her letter?
2 How does she end this (informal) letter?
3 Which expression means 'I'm sorry'?
4 Look at the sentence beginning 'I hope'. Is the grammar the same in your language?

6 Write a letter like Rosie's to John and Steve. Say why you can't go to their party.

7 Look at the picture above. Say what Rosie, Alan and Maria are having for dinner. Do you like this food?

They're having chicken. I (don't) like chicken.

DISCOVERING LANGUAGE

8 When do we use *a lot (of), a little, a few*? Look at the examples in the picture and complete the chart.

COUNTABLE NOUNS	UNCOUNTABLE NOUNS
a lot (of)	....

9 Listen to Rosie, Alan and Maria's conversation and complete the sentences with *a lot of, a little* or *a few*.

1 Maria wants ..... chicken.
2 Alan can have ..... peas.
3 There are ..... potatoes.

10 Work in pairs.

Student A: Cover the picture above. Ask your partner about:
potatoes butter peas carrots bread glasses chicken gravy orange juice

Student B: Look at the picture above. Answer your partner's questions.

A: *Are there many potatoes?*
B: *Yes, there are a lot./No, there are only a few./No, there aren't many.*
A: *Is there much butter?*
B: *Yes, there's a lot./No, there's only a little./No, there isn't much.*

11 Listen again. Complete the sentences.

ROSIE: Would you ...?
MARIA: Yes, please ...

12 Now offer your partner some more of the food in the picture.

A: *Would you like some more chicken, Luisa?*
B: *Yes, please. It's lovely./No, thanks. It was lovely, but I can't eat any more.*

13 Ask your partner to pass you the things on the table in the picture.

A: *Could you pass me the salt, please?*
B: *Yes. Here you are.*
A: *Thanks.*

14 Practise with objects in the class.

Could you pass me that book, please?

Going out for a meal

Focus

- Eating out
- Place settings
- Meals
- Eating times
- Restaurant signs

- Asking permission

- Prepositions: *on* the left/right, *at* the top/bottom, *outside/inside* + place

COMPARING CULTURES

1 Marco is asking his friend Maggie about eating at people's homes in Britain. Listen and answer the questions.

When you go to dinner in another person's home in Britain:

1 Do you take a present? What do you take?
2 Do you arrive exactly on time?
3 What time does the evening usually finish?

2 What is the situation in your country?

3 The text below is about one correct (and very formal) way to lay the table. Match the text with one of the pictures. Then match the things in this picture with these words:

knife fork spoon plate glass

Laying the table

Cutlery

Put forks on the left, and knives (and soup spoons) on the right. The different knives and forks are for the different courses. The small knife and fork are for the first course; the big ones are for the main course, and the small knife on the small plate is for butter or cheese. As a general rule, when you eat you start on the outside and move in to the plate. The spoon and small fork at the top are for dessert.

Plates

The small plate is for bread and is always on the left.

Glasses

There are usually at least two glasses. They are on the right, above the knives.

	at the top	
on the left		on the right
	at the bottom	

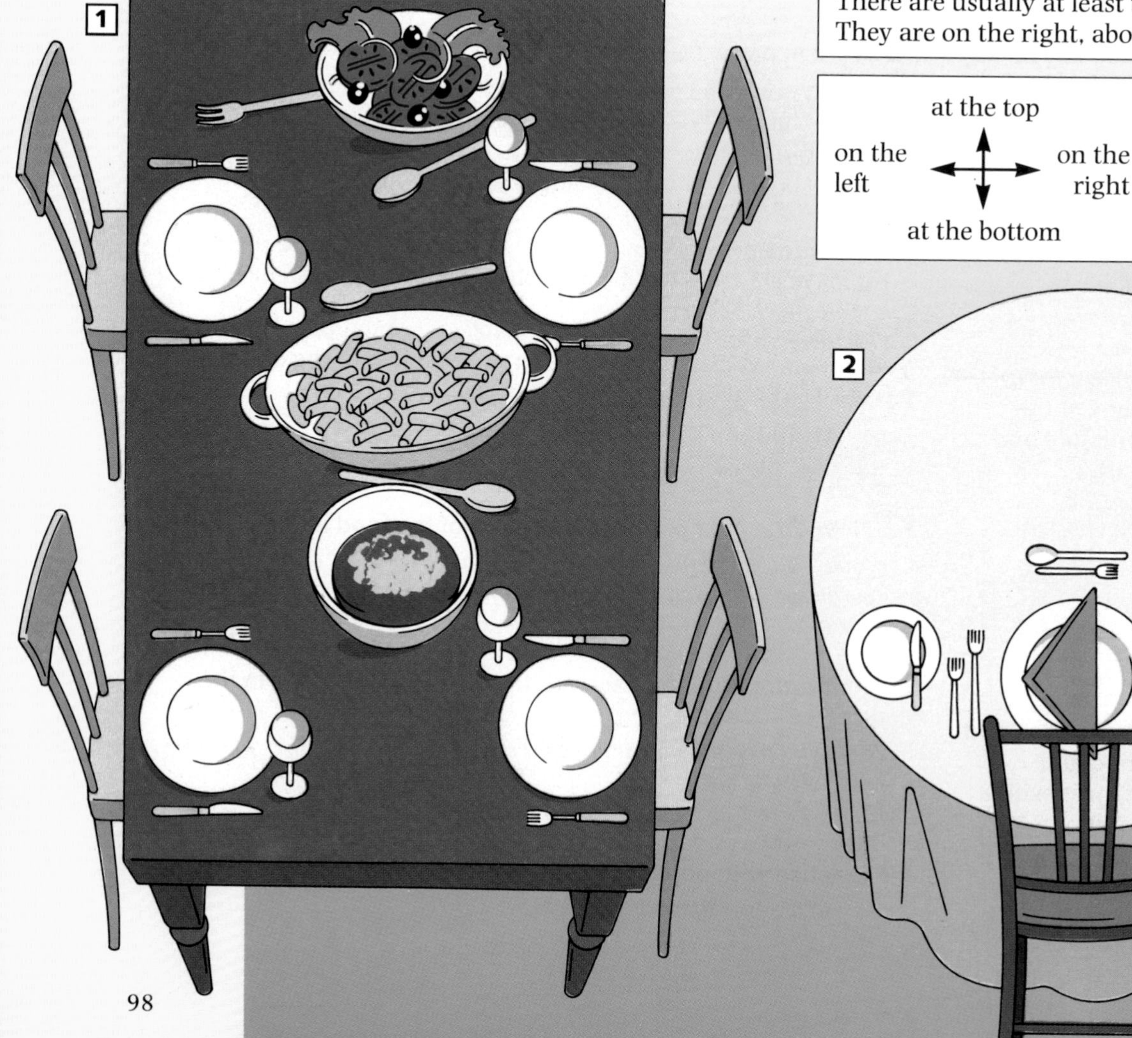

4 **Where can you see a table like this? Describe what you see.**
The chopsticks are at the bottom ...

5 **How do you lay the table for special meals in your country? How do you lay it for family meals at home?**

6 **These items are all from one restaurant. Where exactly do we find them? Match the items with the places.**
Item 1 – on the wall inside the restaurant

on the menu   on the bill
outside the restaurant
on the wall inside the restaurant
just inside the door

1
THANK YOU
FOR NOT
SMOKING
Red House
2
Please ask for our special
children's menu
£1.50
£1.75
£2.50
3
Please
wait
to be
seated
4
Total
Service not
included
5
Opening Hours:
Lunch 12.00 p.m. ~ 3.00 p.m.
Dinner 7.30 p.m ~ 10.30 p.m.

COMPARING CULTURES

7 **Read part of a letter to James from a friend, and complete the chart. Then say when people eat and sleep in Britain and Spain.**
In Britain, people have breakfast at about seven thirty, and they have lunch ...

	BREAKFAST	LUNCH	DINNER	BED
Britain	*7.30*	.....	.....	.....
Spain	.....	.....	.....	.....

2/

I'm in Madrid at the moment, visiting an old friend. It's a lovely city, but I'm having a few problems with the eating times!

At home I usually have a small breakfast at seven thirty, then a sandwich for lunch at about one o'clock. That's OK – it's about the same here. But I always have dinner at about seven in the evening. Not here! In Madrid people usually eat at about ten! In London I'm usually in bed by eleven, but here the streets are full every night until a long time after midnight. My friend says a lot of people go to bed at two or three o'clock in the morning. I don't understand. Everybody is up for work at seven or eight o'clock in the morning. So when do they sleep?

8 **Talk about eating habits in your country. What time do you eat your meals? Which is the most important meal of the day? Do you know other countries where the situation is different?**

9 **Write a paragraph comparing eating and sleeping times in your country with those in Britain.**
In Britain, people ...   In ...

ENGLISH AROUND YOU

Development

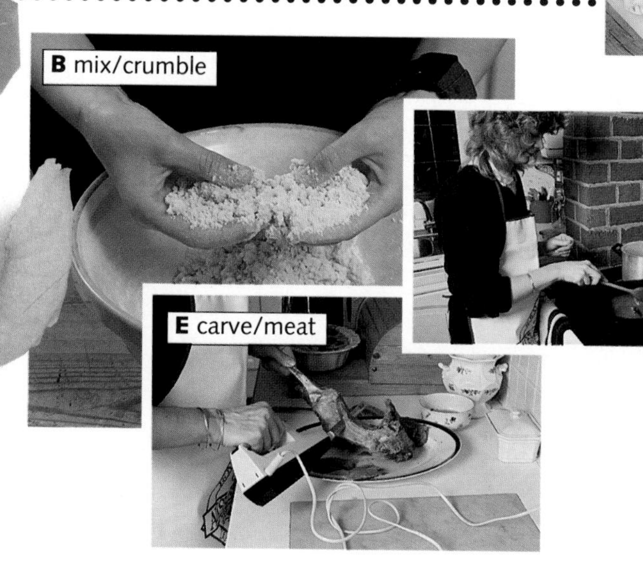

LISTENING

1 Listen to some sounds of cooking. Match the sounds 1–6 with the pictures above. Then say what the cook (Sonia Robertson) is doing in each picture.

1C – She's stirring the gravy.

2 Sunday lunch is an important meal in Britain. Look at the photograph and listen to Sonia. Then answer the questions.

1 Who are the people in the photograph?
2 What are they eating?
3 Who cooks the meal?
4 Why is Sunday lunch a special meal for them?

SPEAKING

3 Talk to your partner. Is there a day in your week when you have a special meal? How many times a week do you cook? Do you like cooking?

READING

4 Here is a recipe for making apple crumble. Match the instructions with the pictures.

1 – Picture B

Apple crumble

INGREDIENTS

225g flour	175g soft brown sugar
75g butter	1 kilo of apples

1. Mix the flour and butter in a bowl.
2. Add 150g of the sugar.
3. Peel and chop the apples.
4. Put them in the bottom of a large dish.
5. Put a little sugar on them.
6. Pour the flour, butter and sugar over the apples.
7. Cook for 30 minutes in the oven at 180°C / 350°F / Gas mark 4.

WRITING: A recipe

5 Think of a dish you can cook. Write instructions for cooking it.

SPEAKING

6 Complete the sentences. Describe your feelings about some aspect of eating or drinking, at home or in restaurants.

1 I love ...

I love { *chocolate.* / *drinking cold orange juice in hot weather.* }

2 I really don't like ...

I really don't like { *cabbage.* / *talking to people at breakfast.* }

Now read your sentences to the class. Give reasons for your feelings.

READING

7 Read the note and answer the questions.

1 What is the purpose of the note?
2 Are Sue and Helen friends? How do you know?
3 Does Sue know what Pat's new job is? Give reasons for your answer.

Dear Sue,
This is just a short note to tell you that Pat got the job! Would you and Jeff like to come to dinner on Saturday evening? We want to celebrate!
Best wishes,
Helen

WRITING: An informal invitation

8 Write a short note inviting friends to your house. Use this information if you want to.

You passed your driving test yesterday. Invite your friends Alan and Jenny to a party at your house on Friday.

Summary

FUNCTIONAL LANGUAGE

Inviting someone
Would you like to have dinner with us?

Accepting invitations
I'd love to. Thanks. / Thank you.

Refusing invitations
I'm afraid I can't come.
I'm sorry, I'm busy.

Thanking someone
Thank you very much for inviting me to your party.

Making polite requests
Could you pass me the salt, please?

Offering
Would you like some more chicken?

Accepting offers
Yes, please.

Refusing offers
No, thank you/thanks.

Talking about quantity
Are there many potatoes?
Yes, there are a lot.

Asking permission
Is it all right if I smoke?

GRAMMAR

A lot (of)/a few/a little/many/much

COUNTABLE	
AFFIRMATIVE	There are a lot of potatoes.
	There are only a few potatoes.
NEGATIVE	There aren't many potatoes.
INTERROGATIVE	Are there many potatoes?
UNCOUNTABLE	
AFFIRMATIVE	There's a lot of cauliflower.
	There's only a little cauliflower.
NEGATIVE	There isn't much cauliflower.
INTERROGATIVE	Is there much cauliflower?

Prepositional phrases
on the left/right
at the top/bottom
outside the restaurant
inside the restaurant

Adverbial phrases
this evening
this weekend
tonight
tomorrow

See the Grammar Reference section at the back of the book for more information.

Directions

Finding your way

Focus

- Buildings
- Street features
- Location

- Giving directions
- Talking about distances
- Further practice: polite requests

- Imperatives
- Prepositions for directions: *on, at, in, across, along, past, into*
- Adverbial phrase: *straight ahead*
- Question: *How far?*

1 Match the pictures below with the places. Which places are not included in the pictures?

Picture 1 – bus station

hospital library petrol station car park
museum police station sports centre
bus station market bank
tourist information centre

2 Listen and list the seven places which the people ask about. Then match the places with the letters on the map above. Before you listen, look at the phrases below.

car park – A

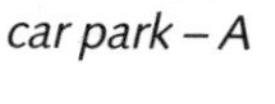

on the corner

in Bridge Street

at the traffic lights

in the square

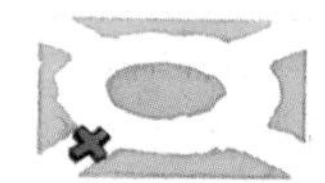

at the roundabout

across the bridge

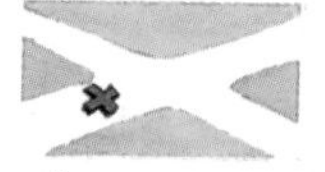

at the crossroads

3 Look at the map. Ask and answer about places.

A: *Excuse me. Is there a car park near here?*
B: *Yes. There's one in Duke Street.*

4 Listen and read. James is going to a meeting, but he doesn't know where the street is. He stops and asks someone. Follow the directions on the map above.

JAMES: Excuse me. How do I get to Bridge Street?

WOMAN: Go straight ahead for about one kilometre. You come to some traffic lights. Turn left at the lights. And the ... first, second, third ... yes, the third on the right is Bridge Street. There's a cinema on the corner.

JAMES: So, it's straight ahead. Left at the lights. It's the third on the right.

5 **Stress and intonation. Listen and underline the words that are stressed in the sentences.**

Go across the bridge.
Turn left at the lights.
There's a cinema on the corner.
It's the third on the right.
Turn right into Maple Road.
Go straight ahead at the crossroads.

Say why we stress these words. Then listen again and repeat.

6 **Work in pairs. Ask and answer about directions.**

Student A: Look at the map and ask your partner for directions to:

1 the sports centre
2 the museum
3 the tourist information centre.

Then give your partner directions to the places he/she asks about.

Student B: Turn to page 121. Give your partner directions.

A: *Excuse me. How do I get to ... ?*
B: *Go straight ahead./Go along this road./Go across the bridge./Go past the bank.*

B: *Excuse me. Could you tell me the way to ... ?*
A: *Turn left/right at the corner/the roundabout. Turn left/right into ... Street. It's the first/second on the left/right.*

7 **Look at the signs. Ask and answer about distances.**

A: *How far is ... ?*
B: *It's about 200 yards/half a mile. It's about ..... minutes on foot/by bus/by train/by car.*

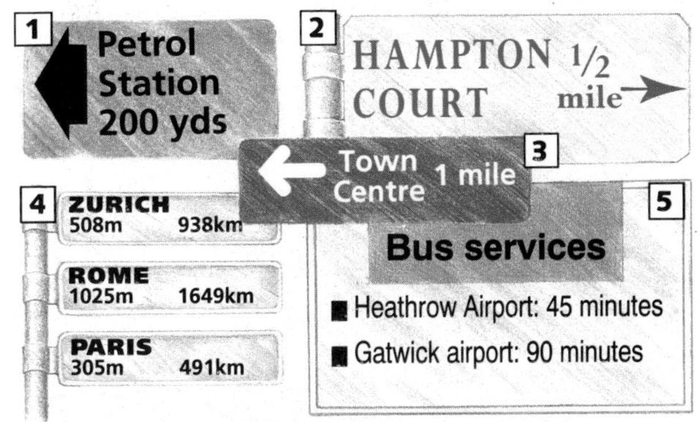

8 **Work with a partner. Think of places in the town where you are studying. Ask for and give directions and distances from your school.**

Is there a ... near here?
How do I get to ... ?
How far is it?

Instructions

This means . . .
– 'don't turn left'.
– 'turn left'.
– 'walk across the road'.
– 'stop your car'.
– 'don't turn right'.
– 'turn right'.
– 'don't walk across the road'.
– 'don't stop your car'.
– 'don't drive into this street'.

Focus

- Signs
- Maps
- Street names

- Giving instructions

- Further practice: imperatives, polite requests, past simple tense

1 Look at the road signs and answer the questions.

1 Which signs are for drivers?
2 Which signs are for people on foot?

2 Match the signs with the driving instructor's words.

Sign 1 – this means 'turn left'.

3 Look at the pictures. What would someone say?

Picture 1 – Please don't park here.

COMPARING CULTURES

4 Read the text about roads in Britain and answer the questions.

In Britain, cars drive on the left-hand side of the road and drivers sit on the right-hand side of the car. Road signs show the distances to towns and cities in miles. Short distances are given in yards.

1 mile = (about) 1.6 km
1 yard = (about) 0.91 m

1 Do cars drive on the left or the right in these countries?
the United States
Hong Kong Sweden
France Brazil Mexico
Malaysia Russia
Japan Australia

2 Do these countries use miles or kilometres?
Australia Egypt
the United States
Italy Canada
India Norway

Now write a similar paragraph about your country.

Maps

1 Look at the pictures below. Why do you think this woman was famous?

2 Read the article about Phyllis Pearsall. Were you correct about her?

3 Are these sentences true or false? Correct the false ones.

1 Phyllis went to school in France.
2 She wrote for a Spanish newspaper.
3 Her husband was a painter.
4 She walked along all the streets of London.
5 She didn't want Trafalgar Square in her book.
6 You can buy an *A–Z* today.

COMPARING CULTURES

4 Street names often describe (A) something in the street (Bridge Street), or (B) a place where people sold food in the past (Bread Street).

Which category are these streets in: (A) or (B)?

Milk Street　School Road　Church Lane
Butter Cross　Castle Street　Fish Street

How do you think these streets got their names?

Long Street　Mandela Street　Trafalgar Square

Now think about street names in your town. Where do they come from?

PROFILE OF

PHYLLIS PEARSALL

by Clare Palmer

Phyllis Pearsall was born in Britain in 1907. She stayed there until she left school, then travelled around France. She earned money by painting people's pictures and writing for a newspaper in Paris. She married an artist and went with him to paint in Spain.

In the 1930s she left Spain and returned to London. She worked for her father's company, making maps of the world. She thought there was a need for new street maps of London and started working on a book of maps.

She collected a lot of information. She walked along every street in the capital and wrote down the name, the important buildings and even the house numbers. She kept the information about the streets on cards in small boxes. One day a box with cards on all the streets beginning with 'Tr' fell out of her window. She found most of the cards, but some landed on top of a bus and she never saw those cards again. When she sent everything to the printer, someone asked her, 'Why isn't Trafalgar Square in your book?' It was because she had lost the card!

'She walked along every street in the capital and wrote down the name, the important buildings and even the house numbers'

She called her book A to Z. The first A to Z was in the shops in 1936 and sold very well. Now it is the most popular book of London street maps. As well as the street names, it shows important buildings like government offices, museums, theatres and schools; parks and public gardens; sports facilities; train and underground stations.

Later Phyllis Pearsall returned to the streets of London to paint pictures of many of the city's famous buildings ■

SPEAKING

1 Elizabeth Moodie, in the photograph above, works in the tourist information centre in Marlow, a town in Britain. What kind of information do you think people ask for?

LISTENING

2 Now listen to Elizabeth Moodie talking about her job. What information do people want? Choose from the list below.

People want information about ...

places to stay sports buying houses
places to visit things to do travel

Were your guesses in Exercise 1 correct?

3 Group the words below under the following headings. Use a dictionary to help you.

PLACES TO STAY	PLACES TO VISIT	SPORTS	TRANSPORT
		football	

football museum horse riding theatre
fishing train castle boat library hotel
swimming caravan bus bicycle sailing
hostel squash guesthouse campsite zoo

4 Listen to two conversations in Marlow tourist information centre. Answer the questions.

CONVERSATION 1

1 Where does this man want to stay?

CONVERSATION 2

2 This man wants to go to the Globe Park ..... Estate.
3 How is he travelling?
4 Follow the directions. Find the place on the map.

5 Work in pairs. You are at the tourist information centre in Marlow.

Student A: You are a visitor to Marlow. Ask your partner for directions to the library and the police station. Then imagine that you work at the centre and answer your partner's questions.
Student B: You work at the centre. Turn to page 122 and give your partner directions.

READING AND WRITING: A booking form

6 You are in Marlow and you want a place to stay. Complete a form like the one below to book a room. Use this information.

You are travelling with two friends. You want to stay in a guesthouse outside Marlow. You want one large room with a private bathroom. You want to eat breakfast in the guesthouse. You plan to stay for three nights. Use your own name, address and telephone number, and today's date.

Date

ACCOMMODATION BOOKING FORM

Name	
Home address	
Telephone	

Number of adults	
Number of children	
Boys	Ages
Girls	Ages

Accommodation required Hotel ☐ Guesthouse ☐ Caravan ☐ Tent ☐
Location
Number of rooms
Type of room
Meals
Number of nights

SPEAKING

7 Work with a partner. A visitor has one day to spend in your town or a town near you. Make a list of the places he/she can see in one day.

WRITING

8 Write instructions for the visitor. Explain how to get from one place to another.

Start at the station. Turn right into Bridge Street and walk to the bus stop. Take the 27 bus to the museum ...

Summary

FUNCTIONAL LANGUAGE

Asking about location
Excuse me. Is there a car park near here?
Yes. There's one in Duke Street.

Asking for directions
Excuse me. How do I get to Bridge Street?
Could you tell me the way to Bridge Street?

Giving directions
Go straight ahead.
Turn left/right.
It's the third on the right.
Go along this road/across the bridge/past the bank.

Talking about distances
How far is the police station?
It's about 500 metres.
It's about ten minutes by car.

Giving instructions
Turn left here.
Don't walk across the road.

Making polite requests
Please don't park here.

GRAMMAR

Imperatives

AFFIRMATIVE	NEGATIVE
go ...	don't go ...
turn left	don't turn right

Prepositional phrases
on the corner/bridge
at the traffic lights/roundabout/crossroads/corner
in Bridge Street
in the square
into Bridge Street
across the bridge/the road
along the road
past the bank

Adverbial phrase
straight ahead

Question words
How far?

See the Grammar Reference section at the back of the book for more information.

15 Future plans

Free time

Focus

- Further practice: spare-time activities

- Making suggestions
- Refusing suggestions
- Accepting suggestions
- Offering
- Talking about future arrangements
- Further practice: inviting, accepting

- *Let's* + infinitive
- Question: *How about . . . ?*
- Modal: *'ll (will)* for offers
- Present progressive tense for future arrangements
- Further practice: *would like* + infinitive

1 **Listen to the conversation between Julia and Anna. Answer the questions.**

1 Is Anna Julia's friend?
2 When do they plan to meet?
3 Where do they plan to go?
4 Who offers to buy the tickets?

Now listen again and complete the conversation.

JULIA: Hello.
ANNA: Hi, Julia. Anna here.
JULIA: Anna! How nice to hear you. (1) . . . . . ?
ANNA: Oh, so-so. And you?
JULIA: The same. Look, Anna (2) . . . . . to go out one evening this week?
ANNA: Julia, (3) . . . . . . When? Which day?
JULIA: How about (4) . . . . . ?
ANNA: I'm afraid I can't tomorrow evening. My parents are coming to see me.
JULIA: Wednesday?
ANNA: Wednesday's fine. (5) . . . . . to do?
JULIA: Let's go to the cinema.
ANNA: The cinema. Great idea!
JULIA: And after that, (6) . . . . . .
ANNA: Wonderful!
JULIA: Right then. I'll (7) . . . . . and I'll call you back.
ANNA: OK. Bye.
JULIA: Bye.

DISCOVERING LANGUAGE

2 **Read the conversation below. Find two ways of making a suggestion and one way of making an offer.**

A: Let's go to the cinema.
B: I'd love to. When?
A: How about tomorrow?
B: I'm afraid I can't. My parents are coming.
A: How about Friday?
B: Yes, that's fine.
A: I'll get the tickets.

3 **Stress and intonation. Listen and repeat.**

Let's go to the cinema. I'd love to.
How about Friday? I'm afraid I can't.
How about tomorrow?

4 **Practise the conversation in Exercise 2, and then make similar conversations.**

1 A: . . . go to a football match.
B: . . .
A: . . . Saturday afternoon?
B: . . . going to a friend's house.
A: . . . next Wednesday?
B: . . .
A: . . . get the tickets.

2 A: . . . go out to lunch.
B: . . .
A: . . . Sunday?
B: . . . visiting my sister.
A: . . . Saturday?
B: . . .
A: . . . book a table.

3 A: . . . have a party.
B: . . .
A: . . . Friday evening?
B: . . . working.
A: . . . Saturday evening.
B: . . .
A: . . . buy the food.

5 **You are one of the people in each of these pictures. Make suggestions for each picture.**

Picture 1 – Let's sit down.

Now offer to do something.

Picture 2 – I'll walk to a garage.

DISCOVERING LANGUAGE

6 **Read the conversation. Is it about the present or the future? Which tense do we use to talk about future arrangements?**

TERESA: What are you doing in the holidays, Jo?
JO: I'm working in a hotel in France.
TERESA: And Cathy? What's she doing?
JO: She's staying at home, I think.

7 **Work in pairs.**

Student A: Look at the pictures below. Ask and answer to complete the information about Teresa's friends.
Student B: Turn to page 122. Answer and ask.

A: *What are Petra and Hans doing in the holidays?*
B: *They're working on a summer camp in the USA. What's Marco doing in the holidays?*
A: *He's . . .*

8 **Look at these notes in Jane's diary for next week. Write about Jane and Teresa's schedule.**

Jane's going to the doctor's on Monday.
They're going on holiday on Tuesday.

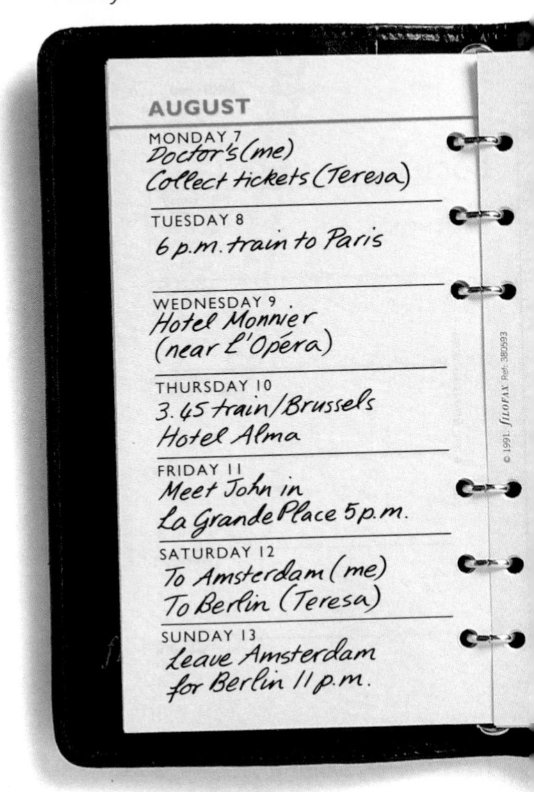

AUGUST
MONDAY 7
Doctor's (me)
Collect tickets (Teresa)
TUESDAY 8
6 p.m. train to Paris
WEDNESDAY 9
Hotel Monnier
(near L'Opéra)
THURSDAY 10
3.45 train/Brussels
Hotel Alma
FRIDAY 11
Meet John in
La Grande Place 5 p.m.
SATURDAY 12
To Amsterdam (me)
To Berlin (Teresa)
SUNDAY 13
Leave Amsterdam
for Berlin 11 p.m.

9 **Ask and answer about your future plans.**

A: *What are you doing this evening/this weekend/in the holidays?*
B: *I'm staying at home/visiting my grandparents/going to Prague.*

Now tell the class about your partner's plans.

Yumiko's going to the cinema with some friends this evening . . .

10 **Listen to James and Julia. Answer the questions.**

1 What is James's question?
2 What is Julia's answer?
3 What is her reason?
4 Is it true?
5 Do you think she is really sorry?

1
West Road
SIX-SCREEN CINEMA WIMBLEDON
Recorded Information 071 328 0701
Performances for Friday 25 October to Thursday 31 October
CAPE FEAR (18)
Fri & Sat 12.00 3.00 6.00 9.00 11.35
Sun–Thurs 12.00 3.30 6.30 9.30
SHINING THROUGH (15)
Fri & Sat 3.10 6.10 9.10 11.55
Sun–Thurs 11.30 3.10 6.10 9.10
FATHER OF THE BRIDE (PG)
Fri & Sat 2.15 4.45 7.45 9.55 12.20
Sun–Thurs 11.30 2.15 4.45 7.45 9.55
SNOW WHITE (U)
Sat & Sun 11.40 2.10 4.40
MY GIRL (PG)
Sat & Sun 1.55 4.30
THE PRINCE OF TIDES (15)
Fri & Sat 1.20 4.05 6.50 9.40
Sun–Thurs 4.05 6.50 9.40
TERMINATOR II (15)
Fri & Sat 11.55

2

The Playhouse Theatre
Wimbledon

Monday 28th October – Saturday 2nd November

British Youth Theatre presents
HAMLET
by William Shakespeare
Directed by Diana Anderson

Evening performances 7.30pm.
Thursday & Saturday matinees 2.30pm.

Prices
Mon–Thurs eves: £10.00/£9.00/£7.00
Fri–Sat eves: £12.00/£10.00/£8.00
Thurs matinee: £7.50/£6.50
Sat matinee: £8.50/£7.50

Hamlet

Focus

- Entertainment
- Booking tickets
- Ways of paying
- Revision of major language items

Booking tickets

1 Choose the correct advertisement.

1 You want to see a play.
2 You want to hear a rock band.
3 You want to see a film.

2 Julia is booking tickets for herself and Anna. They want to see one of the films above – *Father of the Bride*. Read the telephone conversation and imagine what Julia says.

JULIA: Good afternoon. (1) ..... on Wednesday evening?
CLERK: For Wednesday evening? Yes, we have. How many do you want?
JULIA: (2) ......
CLERK: Right. We've got tickets at six pounds and seven pounds fifty. Which would you like?
JULIA: (3) ......
CLERK: OK. Your name, please?
JULIA: (4) ......
CLERK: Right. Please collect and pay for the tickets before seven thirty on Wednesday.
JULIA: (5) ......

Now listen to the conversation and compare your answers with what Julia says.

3 Listen to another telephone conversation. A woman is booking tickets for another of the films above. Complete the chart with the correct booking information.

Film	*Cape Fear*
Day	.....
Time	.....
Number of tickets	.....
Price of each ticket	.....

How does the woman pay?

by cheque
by credit card
in cash

3

DEF LEPPARD
EARLS COURT LONDON
FRIDAY 1st NOVEMBER 7·30p.m.
TICKETS £18·00 and £16·00
CREDIT CARD BOOKING

4 Work in pairs. Look carefully at the advertisements.

Student A: Phone and make a booking for one of the shows.
Student B: You work in a booking agency. Ask for information and complete the booking form for your customer.

Now change roles.

BOOKING FORM			
Theatre/cinema, etc.	.....	Cash/cheque/credit card	.....
Show	.....	Customer's name	.....
Date	.....	Customer's address	.....
Time	.....	Customer's telephone number	.....
Number of tickets	.....	Today's date	.....
Price per ticket	.....		
Total price	.....		

COMPARING CULTURES

5 Look at the key to film certificates below. Talk to your partner. Are there films that children or young people in your country can't see? Who decides what they can and can't see? How do they give this information to the public?

FILM CERTIFICATES (UK)			
U	All ages	**15**	15 years and over
PG	Children with adults	**18**	18 years and over
12	12 years and over		

6 Write about a film or a television programme. Use the example below and these words to help you:

exciting sad dramatic
funny romantic violent
frightening excellent

The Silence of the Lambs is an American film. The main actors are Jodie Foster and Anthony Hopkins. Anthony Hopkins plays a very dangerous criminal. Jodie Foster is a young detective. She asks for his help to catch another criminal. The film is very dramatic and the actors are excellent, but it is not a good film for children.

7 Look at your partner's writing. Ask for more information. Say what you don't understand. Check your partner's grammar, spelling and punctuation.

ENGLISH AROUND YOU

Development

LISTENING

1 Mike Hadley, in the photographs above, is an actor. Listen to him talking about his work. Number the kinds of work below in the order he mentions them.

theatre work – 1

dubbing foreign films theatre work film work television drama television advertisements drama workshops

2 Listen again and say which of these kinds of work:

1 Mike is doing now
2 he did in the past
3 he is doing in the future

3 Listen again and match the expressions he uses with the activities he talks about.

1 'I do games and exercises with children.'
2 'My job is to say the words at exactly the right time so that it looks as if the actors in the film are saying them.'
3 'We did a new play every two weeks!'
4 'You can earn a lot of money doing those.'

a) working in the theatre
b) making television advertisements
c) dubbing a foreign film
d) running a drama workshop

READING

4 Caroline is a young actress. Read the letter from her to her friend David and then complete the chart with her future plans.

MONTH	PLACE	ACTIVITY
March	*Scotland*	*touring*
April	.....	.....
May	.....	.....
	.....	.....
June	.....	.....

5 Now write a letter to a friend telling him/her your plans for the next three or four months.

Dear David,   March 15th

Thanks very much for your letter. Hollywood certainly sounds wonderful!

I'm fine - very busy with "Twelfth Night". Tomorrow we're going up to Scotland: we're touring there for two weeks and then in the north of England for a month. After that I'm having a few days holiday with my mum and dad in Newcastle.

Then on May 10th I'm going to Liverpool for a few days. I've got a part in a TV programme and we're filming it up there. It's my first TV part.

I'm going on holiday in June. Helen and I are going to Italy from June 14th to 28th. We're staying with Francesca in Tuscany. Would you and Debbie like to come? Francesca says the villa's huge. If you'd like to join us, could you write to me at my parents' address? I hope you can come.

Love, Caroline

SPEAKING

6 Read the text. Think about the people and the situation.

It's a cold, windy day. Someone is sitting on a bench in the middle of a park. This person is not doing anything – just sitting and looking straight ahead. There's a small bag on the bench. After a short time, another person comes and sits down at the other end of the bench. The bag is between them.

A: Hello.
B: Oh, hello.
A: It's cold today.
B: Yes, it's very cold.

Work in groups. Describe to each other your ideas about the people and the situation. Then discuss these questions and agree on answers. (There are no correct answers.)

1 Are these people friends or strangers?
2 How old are they?
3 Are they women or men – or girls or boys?
4 What are they wearing?
5 Why are they in the park?
6 Are there other people near them?
7 Is the bag important?

WRITING: A script

7 Now write the conversation between the two people. Remember to write the words the people actually say.

SPEAKING

8 Act your script in your group and make any changes that are necessary. Then perform your script in front of the class. Make it as dramatic as possible!

Summary

FUNCTIONAL LANGUAGE

Making suggestions
Let's go to the cinema.
How about tomorrow?

Refusing suggestions
I'm afraid I can't.

Agreeing to suggestions
I'd love to.
Yes, that's fine.

Offering
I'll get the tickets.

Talking about future arrangements
My parents are coming.
I'm working.
Are you going to the cinema?
What are you doing tomorrow?

Checking telephone numbers
Hello? Is that the Globe Theatre?

GRAMMAR

Present progressive tense for future arrangements

AFFIRMATIVE
I'm working next Saturday.

NEGATIVE
I'm not working tomorrow.

INTERROGATIVE
Are you working tonight?

SHORT ANSWERS
Yes, I am./No, I'm not.

Modal *'ll (will)* for offers
I'll call you back.

Question words
How about ... ?

See the Grammar Reference section at the back of the book for more information.

Progress check 5

Vocabulary

1 Which verb or verbs can you use before each of the nouns?

chop the cabbage

1 chop	the potatoes
2 peel	the coffee
3 wash	the cabbage
4 pour	the butter and sugar
5 boil	the water
6 mix	

2 Write instructions for making a cup of instant coffee.

1 Put some coffee ...

3 Write the names of the buildings or places.

People go there when they want to speak to a police officer. – *police station*

1 Drivers go there to buy petrol.
2 People go there to walk and to look at the flowers.
3 In this building you can see very old things from a lot of places.
4 People go there to watch and listen to actors.
5 You go there to ask for information about a town or place.

4 Complete the sentences with suitable adjectives.

'I cried when I read that book.'
'Yes, it's a very ...... story.'
'Yes, it's a very sad story.'

1 'A lot of people like her.'
'Yes, she's very ......'
2 'I laughed in that film.'
'Yes, it was very ......'
3 'He's got a lot of work today.'
'I know. He's very ......'
4 'Did you watch the late-night film on television? I had to close my eyes!'
'Yes, it was very ......'
5 'A lot of people know his name.'
'Yes, he's very ......'

Grammar and functions

5 Match the phrases with one or both of lists A and B below.

a few – A

a few   a lot (of)   a little   not much   not many

A potatoes   apples   bananas   pieces of cake   packets of sugar

B milk   yoghurt   cheese   sugar   water   flour   butter

6 Complete the answers.

'Are there any seats?'
'Yes, there are ......'
Yes, there are a few.

1 'Are there any seats?'
'Yes, but there aren't ......'

2 'Have you got much work?'
'Yes, I've got ......'

3 'Have you got any money?'
'Yes, but I haven't got ......'

7 Look at the map and complete the sentences with *on, in, of, next to* and *near*.

1 The library is ..... the sports centre.
2 There's a car park ..... the station.
3 The bank is ..... the corner ..... Station Road and Cambridge Road.
4 The police station is ..... the main square.

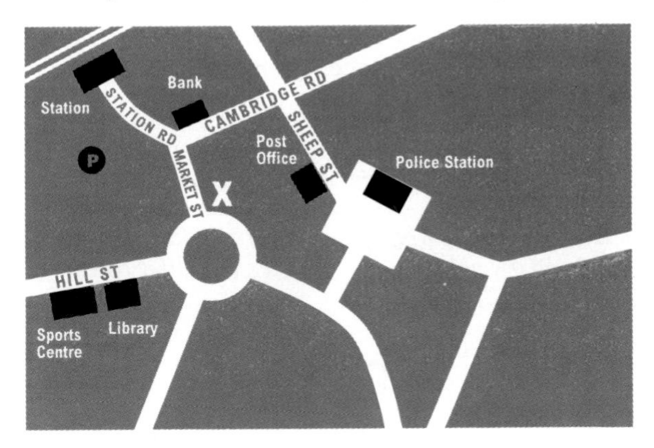

8 Look at the map again. You are here (X). Write directions to the places below.

Go straight ahead. Turn ...

1 the bank
2 the station
3 the post office

9 Match the sentences with the functions.

an offer a suggestion an invitation

1 'Would you like to come to my house for lunch?'
2 'Let's go swimming on Saturday.'
3 'I'll wash the plates if you like.'

10 Match the responses with the sentences in Exercise 9.

a) 'Thanks very much.'
b) 'Thank you. I'd love to.'
c) 'Oh, yes. That's a good idea.'

11 Complete the telephone conversation. You want two tickets for Tuesday evening.

A: Apollo Theatre. Good morning.
B: (1) ..... ?
A: For Tuesday evening? Yes, we have.
B: (2) ..... ?
A: Eight pounds and six pounds.
B: (3) ..... ?
A: Two at six pounds. Certainly. Your name, please?
B: (4) ......
A: And how would you like to pay?
B: (5) ..... ?
A: That's fine.

HOLIDAY PLAN

June 1	Fly to Los Angeles
June 2	Visit Disneyland
June 3	Go round Universal Film Studios
June 4	Drive to San Francisco
June 5	morning: Walk around San Francisco evening: Have a meal in a fish restaurant
June 6	morning: Fly to Arizona Take a coach to the Grand Canyon

12 John is going to the United States next week with a group of other tourists. Write sentences about the first days of his holiday.

On June 1st he is flying to Los Angeles.

Common errors

13 Correct the conversation.

A: Let's to go to the cinema tonight.
B: OK. I love to.
A: I get the tickets.

14 Correct the prepositions.

Turn left **on** the traffic lights.
Turn left at the traffic lights.

1 Go straight **in** this road and **along** the bridge. Go **after** the bank and the station is **in** your right.
2 We can go **to** a walk. Come to my flat first. It's **in** the third floor, **on** the top of the house.

15 Correct the spelling mistakes.

Your homework was excelent. – *excellent*

1 Are you going on foot or by bycicle?
2 We're looking for accomodation in this area.
3 I'm writting to tell you about my new job.
4 Why don't we play tenis and then have lunch?
5 She's realy busy at work today.

At the end of the Progress Check, look back at your mistakes and study the Grammar Reference section if you need more help.

Exercises for Student B

Unit 1 Airport facilities

EXERCISE 8

You are a shop assistant. Your partner is a customer. Sell things to your partner.

Unit 1 Airport facilities

EXERCISE 10

Ask your partner about these objects. Then say if your partner is correct.

B: *Number one. What's this?*
A: *Is it a book?*
B: *Yes, it is. / No, it isn't. It's a passport.*

1 passport

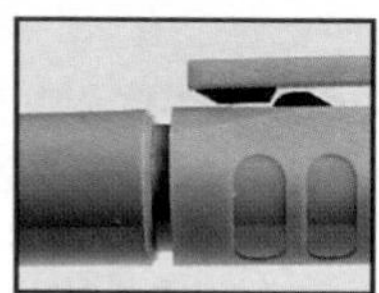

2 pen

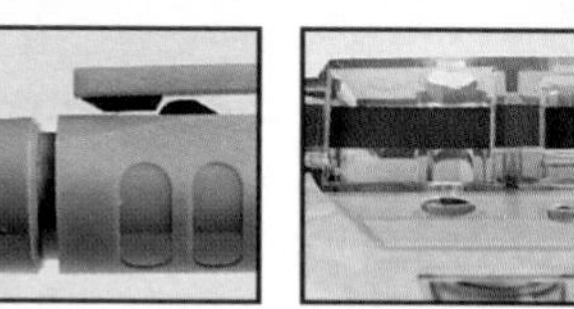

3 cassette

4 bag

5 telephone

6 poster

Unit 1 Development

EXERCISE 3

Look at the pictures below. Answer your partner's question about each place. Then ask your partner about the country.

A: *Number one. What's this?*

B: *It's the Eiffel Tower.*
A: *Yes, that's right.*

B: *Sorry, I don't know.*
A: *It's the Eiffel Tower.*

B: *Where is it?*

A: *It's in France.*
B: *Yes, that's right.*

A: *Sorry, I don't know.*
B: *It's in France.*

1 France

2 Britain

3 the United States

4 China

5 India

6 Japan

Unit 3 Identities

EXERCISE 10

Look at the map of central London and answer your partner's questions about numbers 1, 3 and 5. Then ask your partner about numbers 2, 4 and 6.

A: *Number one. Where are we?*
B: *We're here, in Regent Street.*

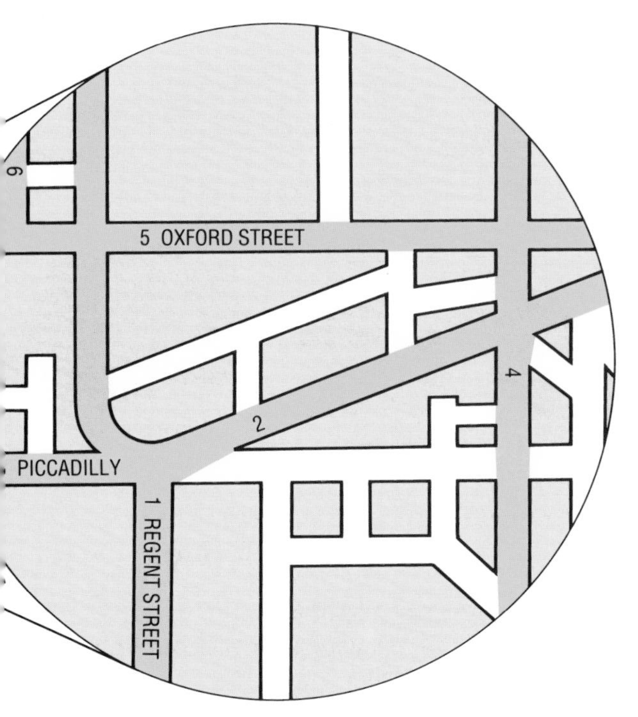

Unit 3 Development

EXERCISE 6

Look at the objects and answer your partner's questions about colours, numbers and prices.

A: *What colour is the library card?*
B: *It's . . .*

Unit 4 Preparing food

EXERCISE 5

Look at the picture. How many differences are there between your picture and your partner's picture? Answer and ask.

A: *In your picture, is there any milk on the table?*
B: *Yes, there is. In your picture, are there any pears in the bowl?*
A: *No, there aren't.*

Unit 4 Preparing food

EXERCISE 10

You are a shop assistant and your partner is a customer. Look at the things in your shop and sell your partner what he/she wants.

A: *I'd like ... Can I have ... ?*
B: *There's some .../I'm sorry, there isn't any ...*

Now change roles and buy the food on your list from Exercise 8.

Unit 5 Possessions

EXERCISE 1

Look at the picture. This is what Alan's got. Say if your partner is correct.

A: *He's got .../Has he got ... ?*
B: *Yes, he has./No, he hasn't.*

Unit 6 Relatives

EXERCISE 7

Ask your partner about Bob Hall.

B: *How old is Bob Hall?*
A: *...*
B: *What does he do?*
A: *...*

1. How old/Bob Hall?
2. What/do?
3. Where/live?
4. Where/work?
5. When/visit/girlfriend?

Now read about Bob's girlfriend and answer your partner's questions.

Penny Harmes is Bob's girlfriend. She's twenty-four. She lives in a flat in Cambridge. She works in a museum. She's the manager of the museum shop.

Unit 7 Buying things

EXERCISE 5

You are a shop assistant in a newsagent's. Your partner is a customer. Look at the picture and then answer your partner's questions.

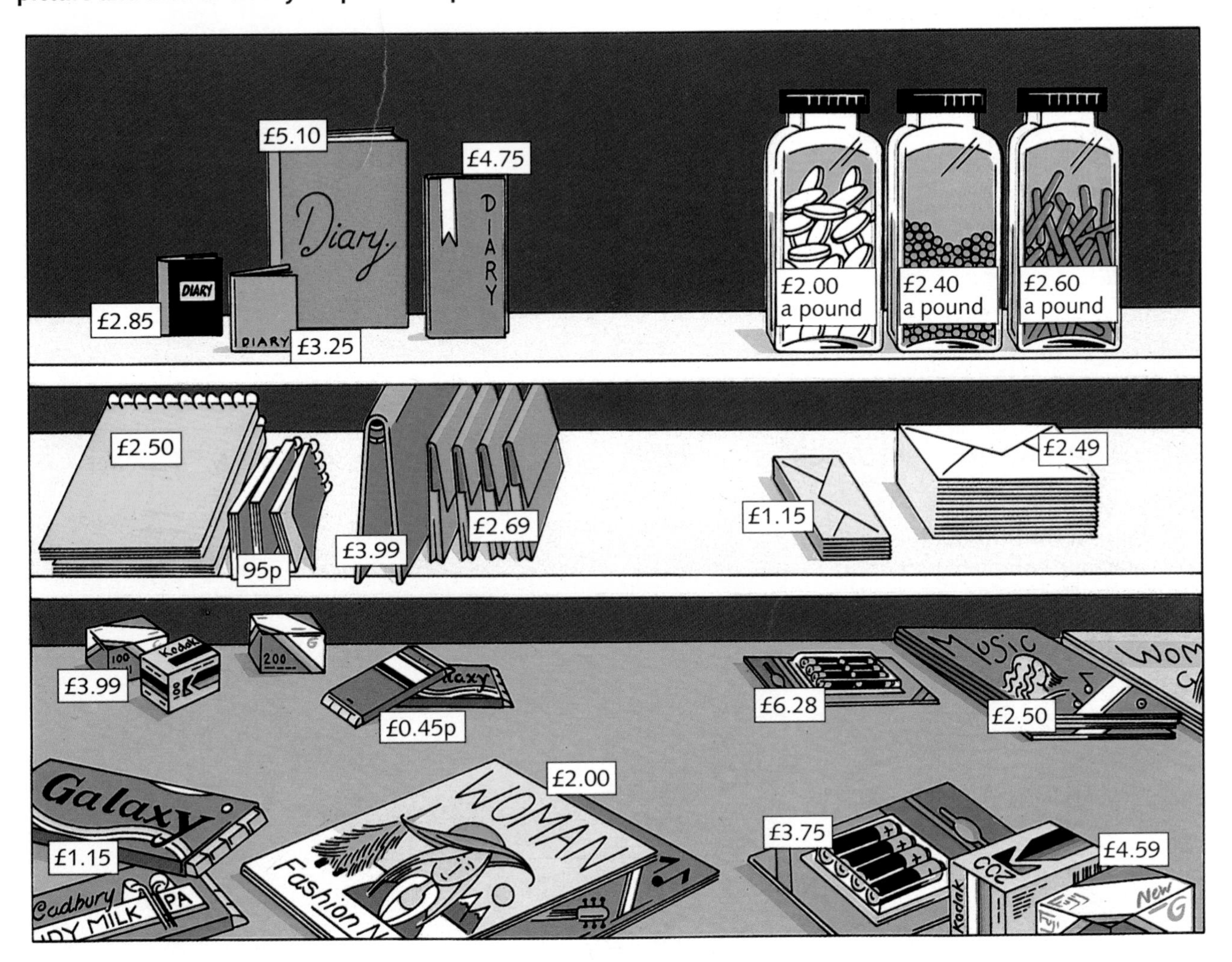

Unit 8 Development

EXERCISE 6

You are the secretary at the Hove International Institute. Your partner wants to study at the Institute and telephones you. Read the information on the right and answer his/her questions. Start like this:

B: *Hello, Hove International Institute. Can I help you?*

A: *Hello. I'd like to do a course at the Institute. Can you give me some information?*

Summer course dates
July 3rd–July 30th
July 31st–August 27th
August 28th–September 24th

Course fees
£1,200 per four-week course (includes accommodation, all meals and the social programme)

Accommodation
Available with a British family or at the Institute

Sports
Tennis, football, swimming, aerobics

Unit 9 Doing things

EXERCISE 5

Look at the picture. Answer and then ask.
Find six differences between this picture and your partner's picture. Use these verbs:

stand talk eat drink carry wear

A: *Is there a man in your picture?*
B: *Yes, there is./No, there isn't.*
A: *Is he standing?*
B: *Yes, he is./No, he isn't.*
A: *What's he carrying?*
B: *A bag.*
A: *What colour is it?*
B: *It's ...*

Unit 11
Yesterday and last week

EXERCISE 4

Look at the information on the map and complete part of the chart. Then answer and ask questions to complete the rest of the chart.

A: *Where was Mike?*
B: *He was in Germany.*
A: *How was the weather?*
B: *It was cloudy.*
A: *What was the temperature?*
B: *It was 19 degrees.*

B: *Where were Rosie and Maria?*
A: *They were in ...*
B: *How ...?*

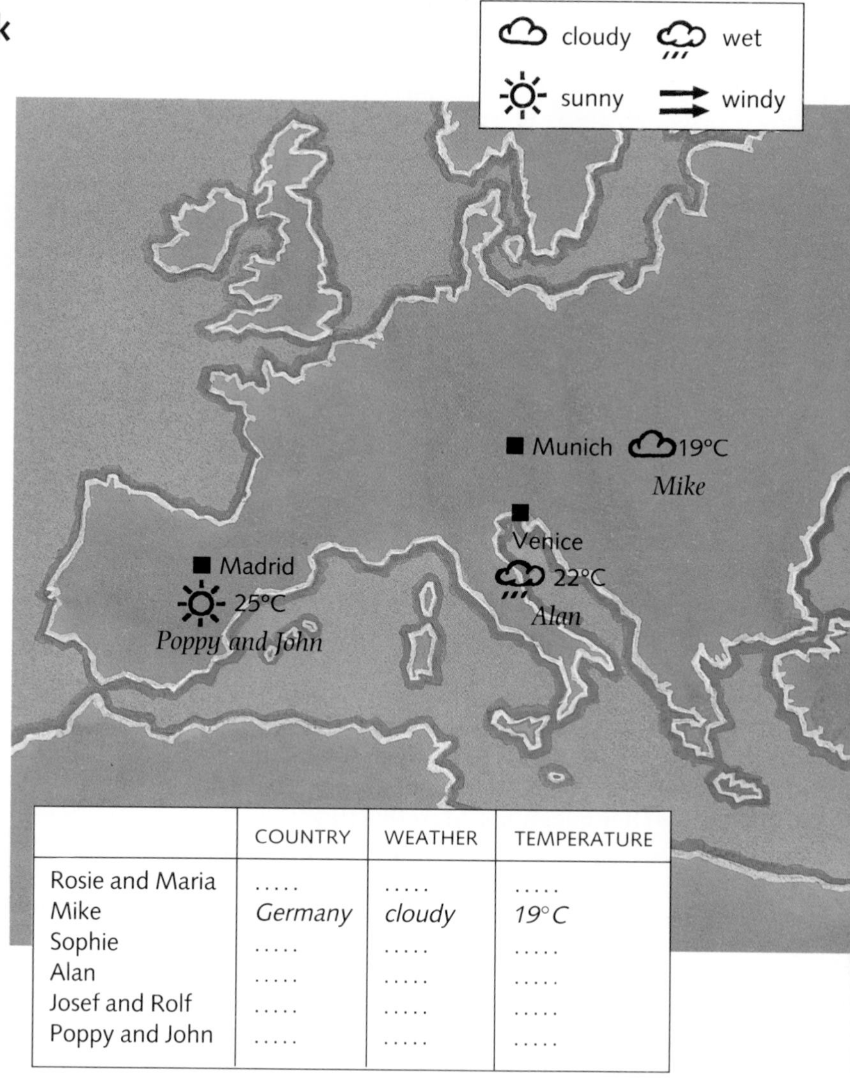

	COUNTRY	WEATHER	TEMPERATURE
Rosie and Maria	.....	.....	.....
Mike	*Germany*	*cloudy*	*19°C*
Sophie	.....	.....	.....
Alan	.....	.....	.....
Josef and Rolf	.....	.....	.....
Poppy and John	.....	.....	.....

Unit 12 Interviews

EXERCISE 10

Read this version of Sarah's interview with Tom Hall. Then answer your partner's questions. Use the information in bold print.

A: *Why did Sarah move to Oxford?*
B: *Because her father ...*

TOM: Right. Your surname is Peters. P-E-T-E-R-S?
SARAH: That's right. Sarah Peters.
TOM: And when were you born, Ms Peters?
SARAH: January 4th, 1973.
TOM: OK. Tell me a little about yourself.
SARAH: Well, I was born in Brighton and I lived there until I was ten. Then we moved to Oxford. **My father got a new job there.**
TOM: Did you stay in Oxford for long?
SARAH: Yes, I did. I stayed there until I left school – that's Fendale Secondary School – at 18.
TOM: What did you study at school?
SARAH: **I studied English, French and Economics.**
TOM: And which college did you go to?
SARAH: The London Business College, and I got a Diploma in Marketing there.
TOM: A Diploma in Marketing.
SARAH: Yes. **I thought that marketing was an interesting subject.**
TOM: Right. And after that? What did you do next? Did you stay in London?
SARAH: No, I didn't. **I finished college in June 1992.** Then I got a job with a hotel group – the TFC Hotel Group – in Liverpool, as a marketing assistant. That was in October 1992. **I worked in the main office. I wrote the publicity for the group. It was a nice job. I liked it.** I left in October 1993 and came back to London.
TOM: I see. Why did you leave?
SARAH: I didn't want to stay in Liverpool. I wanted to work in London.

Unit 14 Finding your way

EXERCISE 6

Look at the map and give your partner directions to the places he/she asks about.

A: *Excuse me. How do I get to ... ?*
B: *Go straight ahead./Go along this road./Go across the bridge./Go past the bank.*

B: *Excuse me. Could you tell me the way to ... ?*
A: *Turn left/right at the corner/the roundabout. Turn left/right into ... Street. It's the first/second on the left/right.*

Now ask for directions to:

1 the library   2 the bus station   3 the market

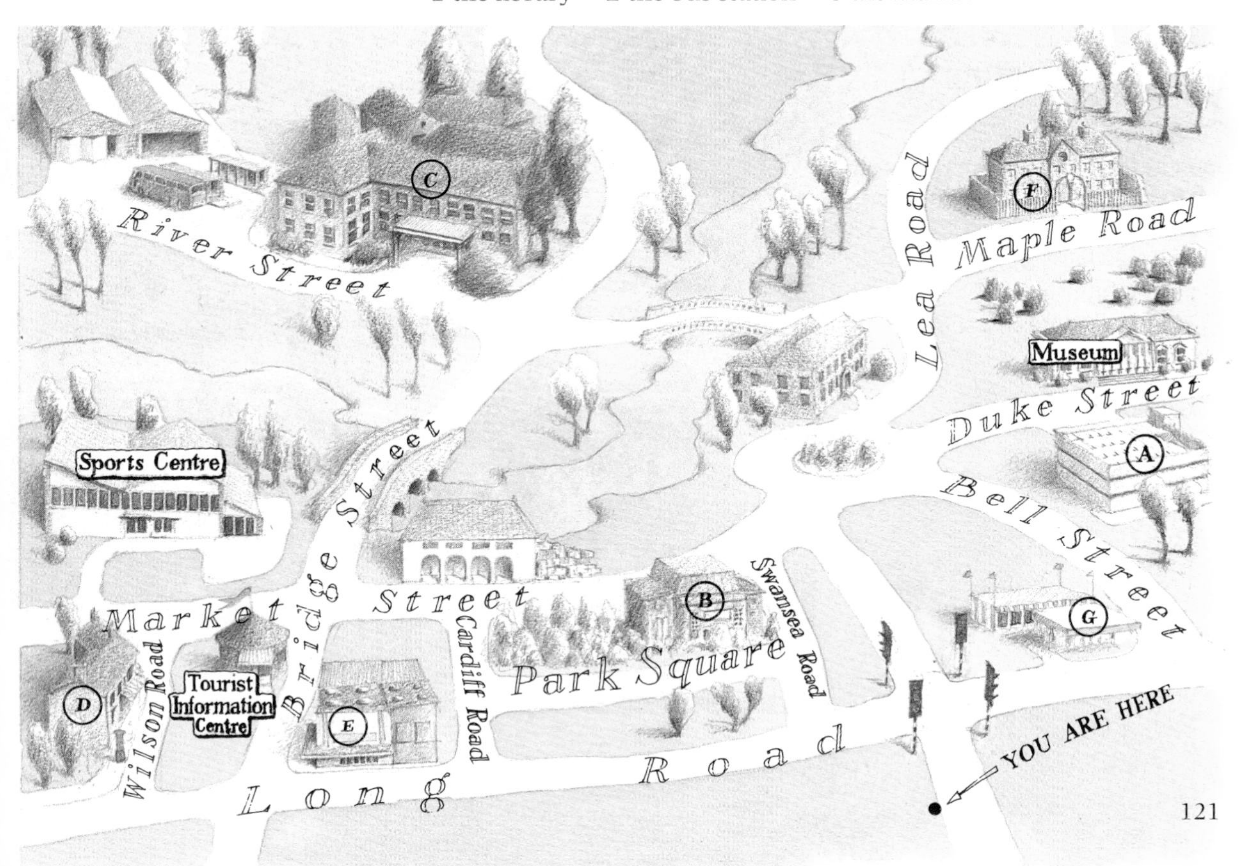

Unit 14 Development

EXERCISE 5

You work at the tourist information centre in Marlow. Your partner is a visitor. Look at the map and give your partner directions.

Then imagine that you are a visitor to Marlow. Ask for directions to the station and the market.

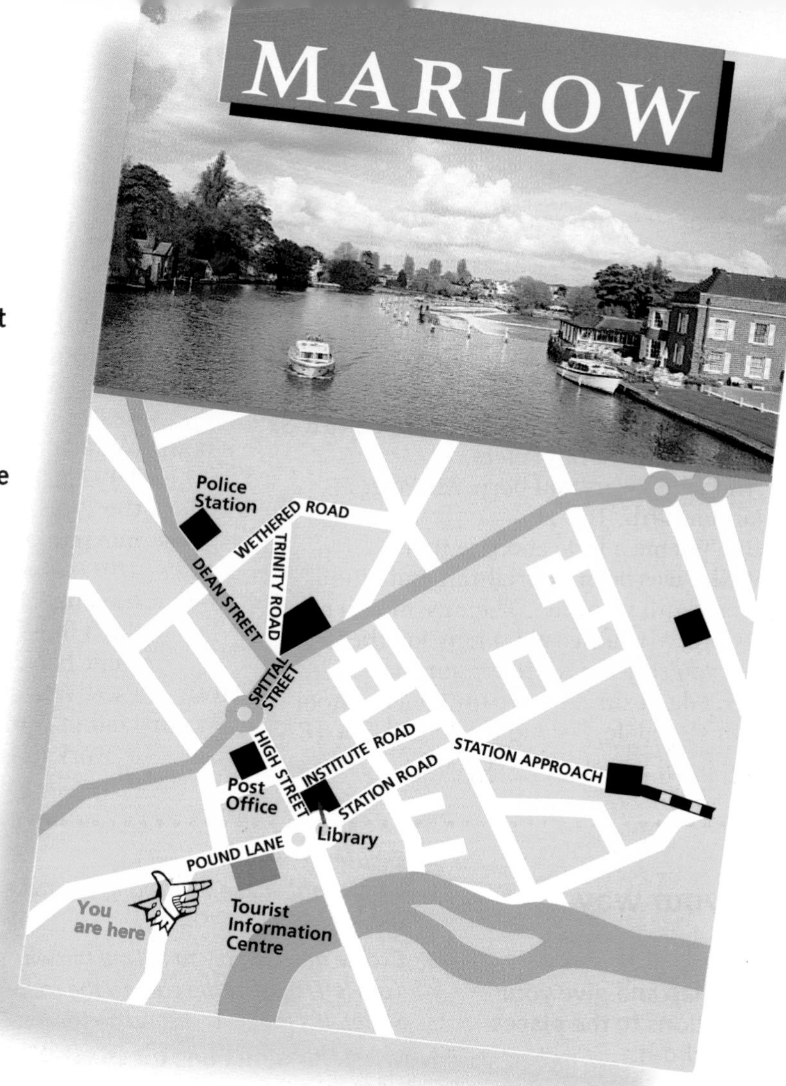

Unit 15 Free time

EXERCISE 7

Look at the pictures. Answer and ask to complete the information about Teresa's friends.

A: *What are Petra and Hans doing in the holidays?*

B: *They're working on a summer camp in the USA. What's Marco doing in the holidays?*

A: *He's . . .*

Grammar reference

This is a summary of the grammar in the book. If a grammar area is difficult for you, read that part of the Grammar Reference. Then look back at the unit in the Students' Book or do some practice exercises in your Workbook.

1 Nouns

Nouns are words which refer to people (*manager*), things (*cassette*), places (*London*), feelings and ideas (*love*). Nouns that are names (of people, countries, towns, companies, etc.) have capital letters (*Elizabeth, Japan, Paris, Texaco*).

1.1 Gender of nouns

Nouns in English do not have gender in the same way as in some other languages. It is only important to know the gender of a noun when you choose a pronoun (*she/her, he/him, it*) or possessive adjective (*her, his, its*) to use with it. Women, girls and (sometimes) female animals are feminine. Men, boys and (sometimes) male animals are masculine. Things, ideas and (usually) animals are neuter. Most nouns that are used for people have the same form for masculine and feminine. Some nouns have different forms:

Examples:

Female:	*sister*	*aunt*	*waitress*	*actress/actor*
Male:	*brother*	*uncle*	*waiter*	*actor*

1.2 Singular and plural (Units 1, 2, 4, 7)

Countable nouns (see 1.3) have singular and plural forms.

a The usual rule for making the plural form is:
singular noun + *s*
Example: *mother – mother**s***

b Some nouns form their plurals in other ways:
- singular noun ending in *s, x, ch, sh*, add *es*
Example: *class – class**es***
- singular noun ending in consonant + *y*, the *y* changes to *i* before adding *es* Example: *country – countr**ies***
- singular noun ending in *f* or *fe* (sometimes) the *fe* changes to *ve* before adding *s*
Example: *knife – kni**ves***
- singular noun ending in *o* (sometimes) add *es*
Example: *tomato – tomato**es***

Some common irregular plural forms are:
man – men *woman – women* *child – children*
person – people *foot – feet* *tooth – teeth*

1.3 Countable and uncountable nouns (Unit 4)

a Countable nouns refer to people or things that you can count. They have a singular and a plural form.
Example: *a computer – two computers*
If the noun is the subject of a verb, the verb is also singular or plural.
Examples: *The girl **is** my sister. The boy**s** **are** my brothers.*

b Uncountable nouns refer to things or ideas that you cannot count. They have no plural form and are not used with the indefinite article (*a/an*).
Example: *food*
If the noun is the subject of a verb, the verb is singular.
Example: *The **soup is** on the table.*

c Some nouns have countable *and* uncountable forms.
Example: *tea*
*Two **teas**, please!* (two cups of tea = countable)
*Would you like some **tea**?* (some tea = uncountable)

2 Pronouns

We use a pronoun in the place of a noun when it is not necessary or possible to be more specific about the identity of a person or thing.

2.1 Subject pronouns (Units 1, 2, 3)

These are the subject of a verb. They usually come before the verb. The subject pronouns are:

SINGULAR	I	you	he	she	it
PLURAL	we	you	they		

Example: *Lola is my friend. **She** is a lovely person.*

2.2 Object pronouns (Unit 10)

These are the object of a verb. They usually come after the verb.

The object pronouns are:

SINGULAR	me	you	him	her	it
PLURAL	us	you	them		

Example: *Here are some chocolates. Do you like **them**?*

a *I/me you he/him she/her we* usually refer to people.

b *It* only refers to a thing or an idea.

c *They/them* refer to people or things.

d *He/him* only refer to boys and men (and male animals).

e *She/her* only refer to girls and women (and female animals).

2.3 *One, ones* (Unit 7)

a We use *one* and *ones* as pronouns to refer to one or more of a number of things.
Examples: *the red* ***one*** *a smaller* ***one*** *this/that* ***one***
the red ***ones*** *smaller* ***ones***

b *One* is also a cardinal number.
Example: *I'd like* ***one*** *green pen, please.*

3 Articles and other determiners

Determiners come before a noun and before adjectives that describe that noun. They limit the meaning of the noun.

3.1 The definite article: *the* (Unit 1)

The definite article refers to one or more specific people, things, feelings or ideas. Its form does not change for singular and plural nouns.
Examples: ***The*** *hotel in Duke Street is* ***the*** *Grand Hotel.*
The *hotels in Thames Street are expensive.*

3.2 The indefinite article: *a/an* (Units 1, 2)

We use the indefinite article before a singular countable noun when we refer to something generally or for the first time. The forms of the article are:

- *a* + consonant
  Examples: ***a*** *mountain* ***a*** *green apple* ***a h****otel*
- *a* + the sound /juː/
  Examples: ***a u****niversity* ***a Eu****ropean country*
- *an* + vowel
  Examples: *a**n a**pple a**n o**range car*
- *an* + silent *h*
  Examples: *a**n h**our*

3.3 The zero article (Units 1, 4, 8)

a We sometimes use a noun without an article when we are speaking generally. These nouns are usually uncountable or plural nouns.
Examples: (U) *Money is important.* (C pl) *Tourists are welcome here.*

b These nouns are usually used without an article:

- countries, towns Examples: *Brazil Paris*
- names of people Examples: *Jane Miss Jones*
- meals Examples: *They are having* ***breakfast.***
- nouns in certain common phrases
  Example: *on foot by car by bus*, etc.
  at home at/to school at/to work in/to bed

3.4 Demonstrative adjectives: *this/that/these/those* (Unit 6)

a *This* and *that* are used with singular or uncountable nouns.
Examples: ***this*** *big house* ***that*** *furniture*

b *These* and *those* are used with plural nouns.
Examples: ***these*** *children* ***those*** *flowers*

c *This* and *these* refer to people and things that are near you (near the place where you are now or near the present time).
Examples: *I'd like* ***this*** *book, please.*
I'm going ***this*** *week.*

d *That* and *those* refer to people and things that are not near you (not near the place where you are now or not near the present time).
Examples: *I'd like* ***that*** *book there.*
The Grand? You stayed in ***that*** *hotel!*

e We also use these words as pronouns, without a noun (see 2.3a).

3.5 *Some/any* (Unit 4)

a We use *some* and *any* with plural nouns and uncountable nouns. They refer to a number of things or a quantity of something which is not specific.
Examples: ***some*** *pens* ***some*** *fruit*

Some is usually used in affirmative statements.
Example: *There are* ***some*** *visitors in the school.*

It is sometimes used in questions when we think the answer is *yes*.
Example: *Can I have* ***some*** *orange juice, please?*

b *We use any* in questions and negative statements.
Examples: Are there **any** glasses?
I haven't got ***any*** *money.*

3.6 *A few/a little/many/much/a lot (of)* (Units 7, 13)

We use these words to refer to quantities of things.

a *A few* and *a little* refer to small quantities.
A few is used with plural nouns.
Example: ***A few*** *students aren't here today.*

A little is used with uncountable nouns.
Example: *There's* ***a little*** *cheese in the fridge.*

b *Many* and *much* refer to large quantities. They are usually used in questions and negative statements.
Many is used with plural nouns.
Examples: *How* ***many*** *children have you got?*
There aren't ***many*** *books in this shop.*

Much is used with uncountable nouns.
Examples: *How* ***much*** *meat did you buy?*
I haven't got ***much*** *money.*

c *A lot of* also refers to large quantities. It is usually used in affirmative statements with plural or uncountable nouns.
Example: ***A lot of** people are coming to our party.*

d We can also use these words as pronouns, without a noun.
Examples: *How much money have you got?*
*I haven't got **much**.* *I've got **a little**.* *I've got **a lot**.*
How many chairs are there?
*There aren't **many**.* *There are **a few**.* *There are **a lot**.*

3.7 Possessive adjectives (Units 1, 2, 3)

Possessive adjectives are used before a noun to show a relationship between one person or thing and another. The form depends on the person or thing that 'possesses' another. The forms are:

SINGULAR my your his her its
PLURAL our your their

Examples: *Is this **your** book?*
*Come and eat at **our** house.*
*The cat is having **its** breakfast.*

4 Possessive *'s* and *s'* (Units 2, 3, 7)

We use the possessive *'s* and *s'* endings, like possessive adjectives (see 3.7), to show a relationship between one person or thing and another.

a *'s* (apostrophe *s*) is added to singular nouns and to plural nouns that do not end in *s*.
Examples: *James is Rosie**'s** brother.*
*Tom is Bob and Lucy**'s** father.*
*I'm looking for men**'s** hats.*
It is often used in the names of shops.
Examples: *the butcher**'s*** *the newsagent**'s***

b *'* (an apostrophe) is added to plural nouns that end in *s*.
Examples: *She goes to a girl**s'** school.*
*These are the cat**s'** bowls.*

c When a person's name ends in *s*, we can add 's or '.
Examples: *Rosie is James**'s** sister.*
or *Rosie is Jame**s'** sister.*

5 Adjectives (Units 3, 6, 11)

Adjectives give us information about a person or thing. They usually come before a noun or after the verb *to be*.
Examples: *It's a **red** dress.*
*It's **red**.*

a Adjectives that refer to size usually come before adjectives that refer to colour.
Example: ***long black** hair*

b When there are two or more adjectives before a noun, you often list the adjectives with commas.
Example: *a **big, blue** boat*

c When there are two or more adjectives after a verb, and they are not followed by a noun, you usually put *and* between the last two adjectives.
Example: *His beard was **long, black and curly.***

For demonstrative adjectives (*this, that,* etc.) see 3.4.
For possessive adjectives (*my, your,* etc.) see 3.7.

6 Verbs

Verbs and verb phrases tell us about actions or states.

6.1 The verb *to be* (Units 1, 2, 3, 11)

USES
We often use the verb *to be* when we give information about the identity or qualities of a person or thing.
Examples: *She **is** a teacher.*
*The dresses **are** expensive.*

FORMS
a *To be* is an irregular verb. Study these forms:

	PRESENT		PAST (NO SHORT FORMS)
	FULL FORMS	SHORT FORMS	
I	am	'm	was
you/we/they	are	're	were
he/she/it	is	's	was

b We form a question by putting the verb before the subject.
Example: ***She is** a teacher.* ***Is she** a teacher?*

c You form a negative statement with *not*. The short form of *not* is *n't*, except after *am/'m*.
Examples: *we**'re not/are not/aren't** German.*
*I**'m not/am not** a musician.*
*He **was not/wasn't** at school yesterday.*

6.2 *There is/are* (Unit 4)

USE
We use *there is/are* to introduce a statement about the existence or location of something. The noun after the verb is the real subject of *to be*; *there* has little meaning.
Examples: ***There is/'s** a postcard for you on the table.*
***There are** ten million people in London.*

FORMS
a We form the question by putting *there* after the verb.
Example: ***There are** two music teachers.*
***Are there** two music teachers?*

b We form the negative by adding *not* or *n't*.
Examples: ***There isn't** any coffee.*
*No, **there is not.***

6.3 The verbs *have got* and *have* (Unit 5)

1 *Have got*

USE

Have got is used in informal British English. It usually expresses possession.

Example: ***I've got*** *a car.*

FORMS

a *Have got* is an irregular verb. Study the forms of the verb:

	FULL FORMS	SHORT FORMS
I/you/we/they he/she/it	have got has got	've got 's got

b We form a question by putting the verb *has/have* before the subject.
Example: ***Have*** *you* ***got*** *a car?*

c We form a negative statement with *not/n't*.
Example: *She* ***has not/hasn't got*** *any brothers.*
Have got is usually used only in the present tense. For other tenses, and the infinitive, the verb *have* is used.

2 *Have*

USES

a In American English, and in formal British English, the verb *have* is used to express possession.
Example: *I* ***have*** *two sisters.*

b *Have* is also used in British and American English for some activities.
Example: *They* ***have*** *breakfast/lunch/dinner early.*

FORMS

We make present and past simple questions and negative statements in the same way as with other regular verbs, using the correct form of the auxiliary *do*.

Examples: ***Do*** *you* ***have*** *a car?*
We ***didn't have*** *any Italian money.*

6.4 The present simple (Units 5, 6, 8)

USES

The present simple is used to talk about:

a a present habit or routine. It is often used with adverbs of frequency.
Examples: *They* ***play*** *tennis at weekends.*
She often ***goes*** *to bed very late.*

b a situation in the present that continues for a long time.
Example: *She* ***lives*** *in Cambridge.*
Note that *She's living in Cambridge* refers to a more temporary period of time.

FORMS

a Study the forms of the verb:
I/you/we/they **work** here.
He/she/it **works** here.

b We form a question with *do* or *does* + infinitive (without *to*):
Do I/you/we/they **live** here?
Does he/she/it **live** here?

c We form a negative statement with *do not/don't* or *does not/doesn't* + infinitive (without *to*):
I/you/we/they **don't swim** here.
He/she/it **doesn't swim** here.

6.5 The present progressive (Units 9, 15)

USES

We use the present progressive (or present continuous) to talk about:

a a present and temporary activity.
Example: *Susan* ***is working*** *at home today.*

b fixed future plans, often with a future time adverbial.
Examples: *When* ***are*** *you* ***going*** *on holiday? We'****re leaving*** *next Tuesday.*

FORMS

a Study the forms of the verb:
I **am playing** in the garden.
You/we/they **are playing** in the garden.
He/she/it **is playing** in the garden.

b The form of the present progressive is: *to be* + present participle (*-ing* form).

c We form a question by putting the correct form of the verb to *be* before the subject.
Examples:
He ***is playing*** *in the garden.*
Is *he* ***playing*** *in the garden?*

d We form a negative statement by adding *not* or *n't* to the correct form of the verb *to be*.
Examples: *They* ***aren't coming*** *tomorrow.*

e We form the present participle in these ways:
- infinitive + *ing*
  Examples: *walk – walk**ing*** *paint – paint**ing***
- infinitive ending in *e*, cut the e and add *ing*
  Examples: *dance – danc**ing*** *make – mak**ing***
- one syllable infinitive ending in one vowel and one consonant, add the same consonant again and add *ing*
  Examples: *stop – stop**ping*** *put – put**ting***
- two or more syllable infinitive ending in one vowel and one consonant, with stress on the last syllable, add the same consonant again and add *ing*
  Examples: *begin – begin**ning*** *refer – refer**ring***
- two or more syllable infinitive ending in one vowel and one *l* add another *l* before adding *ing*
  Example: *travel – travel**ling*** (AmE *travel**ing***)

6.6 The verb *to like* (Unit 9)

After the verb *to like* (and after some other verbs), the object can be a noun or a verb structure. There are three possible structures:

a *like* + noun or noun phrase
Examples: *I like **chocolate**.*
*He likes **coffee with milk**.*

b *like* + gerund
Example: *We all like **swimming**.*

c *like* + infinitive with *to*
Example: *He likes **to have** a large lunch.*

6.7 The modal verb *can* (Units 4, 7, 10)

USES

We use *can*:

a to talk about a person's abilities.
Example: *I **can** drive a car.*

b to ask for something.
Example: ***Can** I have a cup of tea, please?*

FORMS

a *Can* is used with an infinitive (without *to*). Study the form:
I/you/he/she/it/we/they can dance.

b We form the question by putting *can* before the subject.
Example: ***He can** type.*
***Can he** type?*

c We form the negative by adding *not* or *'t*. (Note that *cannot* is one word, not two).
Example: *We **can't** go. People **cannot** understand my French.*

6.8 The modal verb *would* (Units 1, 4, 5, 13)

USES

In this book, we use *would* to:

a talk about something that someone wants.
Example: *Pat **would** like a cup of tea.*

b give an invitation.
Example: ***Would** you like to go to the cinema?*

Would like is more polite than *want*.

FORMS

a In spoken English, *would* usually becomes *'d* after a pronoun in affirmative statements.
Examples: *I'**d** like a cassette, please.*
*We'**d** all like to go.*

b We form the question by putting *would* before the subject.
Examples: ***They would** like some more food.*
***Would they** like some more food?*

c We form the negative by adding *not* or *n't*, but the negative form is not common with these uses of *would*.

6.9 The modal form *'ll* (Units 15)

In this book, we use the short form *'ll (will/shall)* with an infinitive (without *to*) for offers.
Example: *I'**ll help** you.*

6.10 The past simple (Units 11, 12)

USE

We use the past simple to talk about an action, event or state at a specific time in the past. It is often used with a past time adverbial.
Example: *My parents **arrived** in Britain yesterday.*

FORMS

a Study the forms of regular verbs:
I/you/he/she/it/we/they worked
- infinitive + *ed*
Example: *work – work**ed***
- infinitive ending in *e*, add *d*
Example: *like – like**d***
- infinitive ending in *y*, the *y* changes to *i* before adding *es*
Example: *hurry – hurr**ied***
- many short and some long verbs ending in one consonant, repeat the last consonant and add *ed*
Example: *stop – stop**ped***

b Study the forms of some irregular verbs:

INFINITIVE	PAST	INFINITIVE	PAST
be	was/were	meet	met
become	became	pay	paid
begin	began	put	put
bring	brought	read	read
build	built	say	said
buy	bought	see	saw
come	came	sell	sold
do	did	send	sent
drink	drank	shut	shut
drive	drove	sleep	slept
eat	ate	speak	spoke
find	found	spend	spent
get	got	stand	stood
give	gave	take	took
go	went	teach	taught
have	had	tell	told
make	made	think	thought
leave	left	understand	understood
learn	learnt	wear	wore
know	knew	write	wrote
keep	kept		

c We form questions by using *did* and the infinitive (without *to*).
Examples: ***Did** you **like** it?*
***Did** they **go** with you?*

d We form the negative by using *did not* or *didn't* and the infinitive (without + *to*).
Examples: *I **didn't see** any friends. They **did not ask** for coffee.*

6.11 Imperatives (Unit 14)

You use imperative forms to give instructions or advice. The form is the same as the infinitive (without *to*).

Examples: ***Stop! Shut*** *the door!*

You form the negative with *do not* or *don't* and the infinitive (without *to*).

Examples: ***Don't smoke*** *in here, please!*
Do not park *here during the day!*

7 Adverbs

An adverb gives more information about when, how or where something happens.

7.1 Frequency (Unit 8)

USE

We use frequency adverbs to say how often something happens.

Examples: *They* ***often*** *visit Britain.*
We ***never*** *travel by train.*

POSITION

Adverbs of frequency usually come before the main verb.

Example: *We* ***sometimes eat*** *out.*

They come after auxiliary and modal verbs (e.g. *to be, have, can,* etc.).

Examples: *She* ***is always*** *at home in the evening.*
I ***can usually*** *do my homework after school.*

7.2 Degree (Unit 10)

We use these adverbs to describe ability or the extent of an activity. They usually come after the object (or after the verb when there is no object).

Examples: *You can sing* ***well****!*
She can play the guitar a ***little****.*

7.3 Time (Units 11, 12)

We use these adverbs to say when something happens. They usually come at the beginning or (more often) at the end of a clause or sentence.

Examples: *He was at home* ***yesterday****.*
Yesterday *he was at home.*

8 Prepositions (All units)

A preposition comes before a noun or a noun phrase. It usually follows a verb.

Example: *The food was* ***on*** *the table.*

One preposition can have a number of different uses.

Examples: *The food was* ***on*** *the table.*
The meeting is ***on*** *Monday.*

8.1 Place

We use prepositions of place to say where something is or where an activity happens.

Examples: *The bank is* ***between*** *the cafe and the post office.*
I teach Spanish ***at*** *the language school.*

Other common prepositions of place are:

above across along around behind below beside by in in front of into near next to on opposite out of over past round through to towards under

8.2 Time

We use some prepositions to talk about time.

Examples: *We've got visitors* ***in*** *July.*
They're arriving ***on*** *6th July.*

Note these uses of some common prepositions:

- *in* + year, month
  Examples: ***in*** *1996* ***in*** *March*
- *on* + date, day
  Examples: ***on*** *10th January*
  on *Thursday*
- *at* + time of day
  Examples: ***at*** *eight o'clock*
  at *midday*

Other common prepositions of time are:

after before between by during for from past since to until

8.3 After verbs

Some verbs are always followed by a preposition before an object. These verbs can have different meanings with different prepositions.

Examples: ***Look at*** *this picture.*
Look after *the baby; I'm going to the shops for an hour.*